MW00416659

I HOW TO INTERPRET THE BIBLE

HOW TO
INTERPRET
THE
BIBLE

Floyd H. Barackman

KREGEL PUBLICATIONS
Grand Rapids, Michigan 49501

To Ella Myra, my dear wife, a loyal
companion and faithful helper, this book is
affectionately dedicated.

How to Interpret the Bible, by Floyd H. Barackman. © 1989
by Floyd H. Barackman and published in 1991 by Kregel
Publications, a division of Kregel, Inc. P. O. Box 2607,
Grand Rapids, MI 49501. All rights reserved.

Cover Design: Don Ellens

Library of Congress Cataloging-in-Publication Data

Barackman, Floyd H. (Floyd Hays)
   [Practical Bible interpretation]
   How to interpret the Bible / Floyd Hays Barackman.
      p.   cm.
   Reprint. Originally published: Practical Bible
interpretation. 1989.
   Includes bibliographical references.
   1. Bible—Hermeneutics. 2. Bible—Criticism,
interpretation, etc. I. Title.
BS476.B28   1991   220.6'01—dc20   90-20915
                                           CIP

ISBN   0-8254-2280-9 (pbk.)

       1 2 3 4 5 Printing/Year 95 94 93 92 91

Printed in the United States of America

Contents

Preface

We must distinguish between Bible interpretation and Bible study methods. By study methods we look at the Bible from various angles and collect data. By interpretation we analyze this data or the content of a specific passage of Scripture and look for its meaning.

Neither interpretation nor its companion, study methods, is easy. Both require self-discipline and consume time. Because of the persistent opposition of our spiritual enemies as well as the continuing demands of life, we shall always have to give to the study and interpretation of God's Word the priority that the Scriptures deserve. These spiritual exercises never happen of themselves. Our Christian life and ministry depend on this; our knowing God's truth and our pleasing Him require this.

For Bible study methods, a very useful guide is available in *12 Dynamic Bible Study Methods*, by Richard Warren, with William A. Shell (Wheaton, Ill.: Victor Books). For Bible interpretation, I offer *How to Interpret the Bible*. It is written for any Christian who desires to learn how to interpret the Bible for himself. Regardless of the distance one proceeds into this book, he will be a more accurate interpreter of God's Word if he follows its suggestions.

I have taught Bible interpretation (Hermeneutics) at Practical

Bible Training School for more than a decade. My theological posture is biblical, fundamental, dispensational, pretribulational, and moderately Calvinistic. I commend this work to God for His blessing and to His glory.

FLOYD HAYS BARACKMAN

Bible School Park, NY 13737

1

The Bible to Be Interpreted

God has instructed each of us who is saved to read the Scriptures and to allow them to dwell richly in our hearts (Ps. 1:1-3; Col. 3:16). However, this is profitable only when we read with understanding (Acts 8:30). To receive what God has for us from His Word, we must grasp the meaning of what we read. Before we consider how we can lay hold of this meaning, let us first look at the Bible itself.

1. What Is the Bible?

We must accept the Bible as the Word of God if we are to have an accurate understanding of the Scriptures. Many unsaved people regard the Bible to be the product of man, an account of the superstitions and experiences of people who lived long ago. Others who profess to be Christians hold that the Bible is reliable in matters of faith and practice, but not in history or science. Needless to say, this view does not give the Bible the honor it deserves as God's Word. To my mind, it is unthinkable that the spoken and written Word of the infinite, true, all-knowing God should be inaccurate and unreliable.

I hold that the Christian Bible, consisting of the sixty-six canonical books, is God's Word. It is His speaking; it is His message to man (Heb. 1:1-2). In its original production, the Bible was the result of divine inspiration, the product of God's breath (2 Tim. 3:16), the dynamic action of the Holy Spirit (cp. Ps. 33:6; Job

11

26:13) and of His enabling human agents to speak or to write His Word (2 Peter 1:21). Being God's Word, the Bible is inerrant in its content, infallible in its teachings, and authoritative in its declarations and demands.

While God acted upon holy men to produce the *original writings* of the Scriptures, how are we to regard copies of these writings and their translations into other languages such as our English Bible? I believe that these copies and translations are the Word of God in so far as they convey the truth of the original writings. While we do not possess the original writings, we are not at a disadvantage. We virtually know what these documents contained because of the abundance of manuscript evidence.[1] For all practical purposes, the standard editions of the Bible that we have today are the Word of God.

2. What Is the Importance of the Bible?

The Lord's people are aware of the importance of the Scriptures. Being God's Word, the Bible is authoritative in all that it declares and teaches. It not only gives us information about God but also about us and the universe (Heb. 11:3), His provision of salvation (2 Tim. 3:15), and His will for His people (vv. 16-17) and for the lost (John 6:28-29; Isa. 45:22). Also, it reveals important events that will take place in the future.

The Bible gives the answers to the great philosophical questions about the universe, with which darkened human minds have grappled through the centuries. These questions concern *origin* (Where did man come from?), *meaning* (What is man?), *purpose* (Why does man exist?), *relation* (What is man's connection with the rest of the universe?), and *destination* (Where is man going?). In answering these questions, the Scriptures reveal that God created man (Gen. 2:7), that man is a creature made in God's image (1:26-27), that man exists for the glory of God (Isa. 43:7; 1 Cor. 11:7), that man and all that make up the universe have a common Creator (Gen. 1), and that each human being will continue forever, either with God or apart from Him in Hell (Matt. 25:46).

For the *believer* (the born-again Christian) the Bible has practi-

1. See Bruce, F.F. *The Books and the Parchments.* Old Tappan, N.J.: Fleming H.; Revell, chs. 9, 14.

cal application to life. It is *food* for his spiritual nourishment (1 Peter 2:2), a *lamp* for his spiritual guidance (Ps. 119:105), a *weapon* against his spiritual enemies (Eph. 6:17), and the *means* for his knowing and doing God's will (2 Tim. 3:16-17). The Bible not only is instrumental in producing faith (Rom. 10:17) but also works effectively in response to faith (1 Thess. 2:13). Above all, it reveals the truth about the genuine, living God, insofar as He has spoken about Himself.

2

The Interpretation of the Bible

Some people are suspicious of the concept of interpretation, for to them it suggests the idea of manipulating the Scriptures for deceptive or self-serving purposes. In fact, in Bible usage the word "interpretation" means the *explanation* of something (Luke 24:27, "expounded;" John 1:38) or the *translation* of a word or text, that is, putting words into another language (Matt. 1:23; John 1:42). In any case, the meaning of words must be understood before they can be explained or translated.

1. Is There Only One Meaning to the Bible?

Believers who are young in the faith are surprised to learn that good people who know the Lord differ in their understanding of the Scriptures. While all believers agree on what teachings are essential to the Christian faith (the Trinity, the deity of Christ, etc.), not all have identical understanding of these doctrines. Although it may have many applications, any particular passage or statement in the Bible ideally has only one meaning. However, in real life godly believers are unable to agree on what this meaning is regarding many passages of Scripture.

What accounts for this when we all are taught by God the Holy Spirit? In seeking the meaning of a passage, we bring to this interpretation process certain elements that are defective. *Incomplete or are imperfect* These elements include our understanding of the meaning of words, our overall grasp of the Scriptures, our religious training

14

and conditioning, and our life experience. The input of these elements introduces faulty features into our understanding of God's Word.

Because of this, all present human understanding of the Scriptures is relative. This means that this understanding is not the same for all people and that it is subject to change as we grow in spiritual life and knowledge (Col. 1:10; 2 Peter 3:18). Furthermore, the Holy Spirit teaches each child of God according to his spiritual development, need and ministry. In the process of our spiritual development, the Holy Spirit gradually corrects the defective elements we bring to Bible interpretation and gives us new insight into God's Word. This process continues throughout our lives.

Since we are not all at the same level of spiritual development and do not bring to Bible interpretation the same elements of understanding, there cannot now be one meaning on which all believers agree in every detail. The meaning which we grasp, with dependence upon the Holy Spirit and by application of the rules of interpretation, is the one that God has for us at our present stage of spiritual development and for our ministry. With additional insight and with the correction of our faulty human input, our understanding of biblical truth constantly widens and deepens and becomes more accurate.

As much as possible, we must avoid subjectivism when we interpret the Scriptures. Subjectivism is the deliberate distortion of the ordinary meaning of Scripture to suit one's interests or preferences. We must permit the Bible to speak for itself rather than allow religious bias or preconceived ideas to control our interpretation.

2. What Are Some Requirements for Interpreting the Bible?

(1) *We must be born again.*

Besides receiving the divine resident Teacher, the Holy Spirit, the born-again person also experiences the renewing of his soul and spirit, the seat of understanding, which gives him the capacity to understand spiritual truth (Eph. 4:23).

(2) *We must accept the divine origin and authority of the Bible as well as the infallibility of its teachings.*

Only as we honor the Scriptures as being the very, and inerrant, Word of God, will we be taught by God.

(3) *We must have the confidence that accurate translations of the Scriptures convey the essential meaning of the Bible.*

While a knowledge of the Hebrew and Greek languages in which the original documents were written is helpful, this knowledge is not indispensable to practical Bible interpretation. Highly accurate literal translations of the Bible, such as the King James Version, the New King James Version, the American Standard Version (1901), and the New American Standard Version, are sufficient.

(4) *We must believe in the unity of the Scriptures and in their progressive record of divine truth.*

This means that there is perfect agreement among the parts of the Scriptures as well as progression in their revelation of truth.

(5) *We must accept the fact that the Bible often is its own interpreter.*

We must see if this biblical interpretation exists before constructing our own interpretation of a passage.

(6) *We must believe that the Bible means what it says according to the literal, biblical usage of its words.*

We must interpret all Scripture literally, according to the biblical usage of its words, and recognize the literal truth that figurative expressions convey.

(7) *We must be willing to respond to God's Word in a suitable way* (John 8:31-32).   Luke 8:18

See Chapter 3, (6). This response will be governed by our motivations and attitudes.

3. Do We Need Human Teachers of the Bible?

The apostle John writes, "Ye need not that any man teach you" (1 John 2:27). On the other hand, the Lord has given to the Church human teachers (Eph. 4:11), who have the gift of teaching (1 Cor. 12:28). When they are prepared by study and are divinely enabled by the Spirit of God, these people can clearly and effectively explain to others God's Truth. This teaching ministry allows to others who are not teachers the time to pursue their own special ministries in the Church.

Still, it is the duty of every believer to search out and understand the Word of God for himself, even when he is taught by others (Acts 17:10-11; 2 Tim. 2:15). We should not be wholly dependent upon teachers for our understanding of the Bible. They are divinely given to help our understanding, not control it. John appears to be saying that having the Holy Spirit as our Teacher, we are not at the mercy of human instructors.

4. What Are Some Aids for Bible Interpretation?

(See Appendix D for a list of titles.)

(1) *A study Bible, preferably one with wide margins or interleaved blank pages for writing notes.*

A working Bible with published comments is not so desirable since we are seeking our own understanding of the Scriptures rather than that of others. On the other hand, an annotated Bible is profitable for reference when it is used discriminately. (See Appendix G.)

(2) *A complete concordance of the Bible in the version that will be used.*

A concordance is a list of biblical words in alphabetical order and with references to their locations. A concordance which has all the words in the version of the Bible that one is interpreting is most useful.

(3) *A Bible cross-reference book.*

The Treasury of Scripture Knowledge, which has some 500,000 references to other passages in the Bible, is very helpful.

(4) *Books dealing with biblical words and their meanings in the Scriptures.*

These include dictionaries and word-study books.

(5) *Commentaries, written by godly, reliable writers.*

Except for word studies, one should consult the understanding of others last in the interpretation process. As far as possible, we want to avoid depending on the opinions of others for our understanding of the Bible. On the other hand, we should not ignore what the Holy Spirit has taught others. Also, many commentaries have textual and background information that is helpful to interpretation. When we consult the comments of others, we must not adopt their views without being sure that they are in harmony with the general teachings of the Bible.

3

Our Divine Teacher

One of the ministries of the Holy Spirit is to teach us the things of God, given in the Scriptures (John 14:26). In 1 John 2:27, He is referred to as the Anointing who teaches us all things.

1. The Need For His Teaching Ministry (1 Cor. 2:7-12)

(1) *God's Truth is beyond unaided human understanding* (v. 7).

Paul speaks of God's Truth ("wisdom") as a "mystery." In the New Testament a mystery is divine truth that is hidden from the world and is revealed to God's people (Eph. 3:3, 5). Being divinely hidden, God's Truth cannot be understood by the world (1 Cor. 2:7-9). Although it is divinely revealed to His people, God's truth is still beyond our unaided understanding, for He is far greater than we creatures.

(2) *God's Truth cannot be known by the means men ordinarily use to acquire knowledge* (vv. 9-10a).

The world acquires knowledge by the scientific method, which involves observation, theorizing, and testing. But spiritual reality cannot be studied by this method, which applies only to the physical aspects of the universe.

How, then, does the believer know that there is something beyond the physical realm? By divine revelation (10a). God speaks in His Word about the things that exist beyond the reach of scientific instruments. Thus the things of God are to be received by faith in His revelation (Heb. 11:3). God's Word is more certain than those things which we can detect with the physical senses (2 Peter 1:16-19).

(3) *Only the Holy Spirit understands God's Truth* (vv. 10b-12)

Being the Third Person of the Holy Trinity, the Holy Spirit searches the deep things of God (10b). Paul declares that, as we humans have a human spirit which enables us to understand human affairs, so having the Holy Spirit we believers can understand the things of God (11-12). The unsaved do not understand the things of God (His Truth), for they do not have the Holy Spirit to teach them (John 14:17) and they are blinded to God's truth (2 Cor. 4:4; Eph. 4:17-18).

2. The Fact of His Teaching Ministry (1 Cor. 2:12-13)

(1) *Having the Holy Spirit, we are taught by Him* (v. 12).

We received the Holy Spirit when we trusted the Lord Jesus as our Savior (1 John 4:13). Because of His abiding presence in us, the Holy Spirit is always ready to teach us, as the Lord promised (John 14:26).

(2) *The Holy Spirit uses the Scriptures to teach us* (v. 13).

The Holy Spirit teaches us the deep things of God by means of the Scriptures, such as that which Paul spoke and wrote. It is an inexpressible privilege and blessing to possess God's Word in our language.

3. The Requirements For Our Receiving His Teaching Ministry

To receive the teaching ministry of the Holy Spirit, we must . . .

(1) *Give ourselves to His influence and work* (Eph. 5:18).

Paul appeals to his Christian readers to be filled with the Holy Spirit. This is not to receive more of Him but to come under His influence. We experience His filling when we cooperate with Him in a way which will allow Him to help us. This relationship demands that we deal with known sins in our lives by repentance and confession to God (Eph. 4:30; Rev. 2:5; 1 John 1:9), that we yield ourself to God's management and direction (1 Thess. 5:19; Matt. 11:29), and that we depend upon Him to do

Gal. 5:16

His work as we do ours (John 7:37-39; Gal. 2:20; Acts 6:5). When we adjust ourself to the Spirit's presence in this way, we allow Him to teach us.

(2) *Pray to Him* (Ps. 119:18).

Some may object to praying to the Holy Spirit, but there is no scriptural prohibition against this. He is our Helper, with whom we can have fellowship (John 14:16; 2 Cor. 13:14). Also, prayer is necessary if we are to receive divine help (James 4:2). We must develop the habit of looking to the Holy Spirit to give us understanding whenever we read or hear God's Word.

(3) *Be rightly motivated* (John 7:16-17).

Some read the Scriptures to satisfy their curiosity or to find support for some argument. But a better purpose is the desire to learn about God and His will for us for better worship and obedience (Deut. 29:29).

(4) *Read and meditate upon the Word* (Ps. 1:1-3; Col. 3:16).

The Holy Spirit can teach us only as we give our minds and hearts to that medium which He uses, the Word of God.

(5) *Apply the rules of Bible interpretation.*

These rules guide us in our understanding of a passage by suggesting procedures to follow in the interpretation process.

(6) *Rightly respond to God's Word* (Luke 8:18).

An appropriate response to the Word allows our under-standing of it and our retention of what we have learned. As we shall see, it is especially important for us to heed the instructions that are given in the New Testament since this portion of the Bible is the dispensation which God has given His people to follow today. *you either gain or lose you cannot stand still*

Appropriate responses to the Scriptures are these: If it is a *warning*, heed it; a *failure*, confess it; a *direction*, follow it; a *rebuke*, accept it; a *teaching*, receive it; or a *blessing*, give thanks for it.

(7) Use *sound tools.*

Some titles of helpful books are given in Appendix D. Certain books, like concordances, word-study books, and dictio-naries, are essential to interpretation. On the other hand, the opinions of Bible teachers, given in commentaries, are useful, but they must be treated cautiously. While we should not rely on others to think for us, we should not ignore what God has taught them. We can learn from them as we look at their insights in the light of the Word (Acts 17:11). The trustworthiness of a book or tape may be determined by the reputation of its author and publisher and by its loyalty to the doctrines of the Bible.

4. The Effectiveness of His Teaching Ministry

The effectiveness of the Holy Spirit's teaching ministry is indicated by John's words, "as He has taught you" (1 John 2:27). The experience of a host of believers demonstrates that the Holy Spirit is an effective teacher and that His teaching ministry is absolutely indispensable for our understanding of God's Word.

5. Our Duty Because of His Teaching Ministry

Having been taught by the Holy Spirit, our duty is to apply the truth we have learned to our own lives (James 1:22-25; 4:17). Also, we must share with others what we have learned for their edification and ministry (2 Tim. 2:2; Eph. 4:29).

In view of the teaching ministry of the Holy Spirit, it is important for us to cultivate our relationship with Him. This will allow Him not only to teach us but also to help us to be and to do all that God desires for us. Remember to look to this wonderful Helper to teach you. As we ask Him to do this we must trust Him to do so (Ps. 119:18).

4

Rules for Interpreting the Bible

1. A Description of Context

The context of a <u>text</u>, or passage, to be interpreted is what <u>precedes</u> and what <u>follows it</u>.

2. The Kinds of Context

(1) The <u>immediate</u> context

This consists of what directly precedes and/or follows the passage that is to be interpreted. The limits of the immediate context are determined by the limits of the principal thought, activity, or topic of which the passage to be interpreted speaks.

For example, Philippians 4:19 is found in an immediate context of verses 18-19, in which Paul gives assurance to his readers that he has everything he needs (18) and that God will provide for their needs (19). The principal thought here is assurance.

(2) The <u>larger</u> context

This consists of a larger section of the book or Psalm, of which the immediate context is a subdivision. Again, the limits of the larger context are determined by a single theme.

For example, the larger context of Philippians 4:19 is verses 10-20. The theme of this passage is "Paul's Acknowledgment of the Philippians' Gifts" (4:10-20). An outline follows:

A. Paul's rejoicing (4:10-17)
   a. The expression of his joy (10)
       (a) Statement (10*a*)
       (b) Reason (10*b*)
   b. The motivation for his joy (11-17)
       (a) Not the provision of his needs (11-13)
           a) Statement (11a)
           b) Explanation (11*b*-13)
       (b) Their opportunity to minister (14-17)
           a) Statement (14)
           b) Explanation (15-17)
B. His assuring his readers (18-19)
   a. That he has everything he needs (18).
   b. That God will provide for their needs (19).
C. His praising God (20).

3. Observe that this larger context, Philippians 4:10-20, is a major division of this book, as follows:

A. Paul's salutation (1:1-2)
B. His thanksgiving and praise (1:3-11)
C. His circumstances (1:12-26)
D. His exhortations (1:27—2:18)
E. His future plans (2:19-30)
F. His warning against false teachers (3:1—4:1)
G. His final exhortations (4:2-9)
H. His acknowledgment of their gifts (4:10-20)
I. His farewell (4:21-23)

3. The Importance of the Context

Interpreting a text, or a passage, according to its context contributes to the accuracy of the interpretation. As the proper place, with its context, gives meaning to a piece of a jigsaw puzzle, so the context gives meaning to a text and ties it to the rest of the Scriptures.

Apart from its context, a text might mean anything that one might imagine. For example, we read in the Bible, "There is no

words pharses + closses can have multible meanings
Thoughts are usually expressed in a series of words + sentences
False interpetations arise from inoring the context

God." But in context, we read, "The fool hath said in his heart, 'There is no God' (Ps. 14:1).

4. The Procedure in Applying This Rule

Seek answers to the following questions:

(1) What is the immediate context of the passage to be interpreted and its theme?
(2) What is the larger context of the passage to be interpreted and its theme?
(3) Who is writing and/or speaking?
(4) Who is being addressed?
(5) What does the context contribute to the passage being interpreted?
(6) What does the passage being interpreted say in the light of its context? (Give a summary statement.)

skip
~~(7)~~ What does the passage being interpreted contribute to the context and to its theme?

5. An Example of This Rule

Using Philippians 4:19 as a text to be interpreted according to its context, let us seek answers to the questions of Section 4.

Question 1: The immediate context is vv. 18-19. "Assurance." (See Sec. 2, (1).)

Question 2: The larger context is verses 10-20. The theme is The theme is "Paul's Acknowledgment of the Philippians' Gifts." (See Sec. 2, (2).)

Question 3: The writer is the apostle Paul (1:1, 3).

Question 4: The addressees are the believers at Philippi (1:1).

Question 5: The context tells why God will provide for the material needs of the Philippians (vv. 14-18). They had been generous toward Paul.

Question 6: In the light of the context, the text assures that God will provide for the Philippians' material needs since they were mindful of Paul's needs.

Question 7: Paul assures his readers that God will make up for any lack that they may have incurred because of their generosity toward him.

6. An Exercise

Following the procedure in Section 4, interpret John 9:3 and Daniel 6:4. Were these people sinless? Jn 15:6

RULE TWO: *Interpret the passage in the light of all that the Bible teaches.*

---

1. An Explanation

The whole Bible is the *ultimate context* of any biblical passage. Since the Scriptures are the Word of God, we find a consistency in their teachings throughout the Bible. God does not say something in one place and contradict Himself in another.

The principle of the self-consistency of the Scriptures is this: There is in the Bible perfect agreement among the parts that comprise the whole revelation of divine truth. Because the whole biblical revelation of a specific teaching exceeds that which any single passage gives, we should seek to understand what all the Bible says about this topic.

People who hold an unbiblical view of a doctrine often do so because their view is based on only part of what the Bible says about the doctrine, not on all that it says. To be accurate interpreters of the Word, we must search out and learn what all the Bible teaches about a subject.

2. The Procedure in Applying This Rule

To learn what meaning the Bible as a whole gives to the passage being interpreted, follow these steps.

(1) After studying the passage in its context, list the truths, or topics, of the passage as they are expressed by key words and ideas.

(2) See how *if* these topics, expressed by their key words and ideas, occur elsewhere in the Bible and what additional information these passages give about these topics.

> 1) Consult a complete concordance of the Bible version you are using to learn if these topics, expressed by key words, occur elsewhere in the Scriptures. Use a topical concordance of the Bible for references to the ideas that

express these themes. Also, look up the cross-references in the margin of your Bible or in *The Treasury of Scripture Knowledge*.

(2) Study these references in their complete contexts to learn what light they cast on the topics that are mentioned in the passage you are interpreting.

(3) In the light of the information you have gathered in your research, decide what facts particularly relate to the topics expressed in the passage being interpreted.

(4) In the case of more than one biblical interpretation, select the one that best fits the topic and its context.

(5) Consider the understanding that this selected biblical data gives to the topics in the passage. Be sure that your interpretation of these topics, in the light of what the Bible teaches elsewhere, is in harmony with their contexts. (Note: Always interpret obscure statements by truth that is clearly taught elsewhere in the Bible.)

3. An Example of This Rule

According to the procedure in Section 2, let us interpret these words of the Lord Jesus in the light of their context and general Bible teaching:

"Except a man be born of water and of the Spirit" (John 3:5)

(1) We learn from the context that the Lord Jesus is speaking about the new birth (6-7). The question under consideration is the meaning of the words, "be born of water." Do these words refer to water baptism and teach that this rite is necessary for the new birth? Also, what is the meaning of "Spirit"?

(2) Elsewhere in the Bible we learn the following about the new birth, water, and the Spirit:

One, for other passages on the subject of the new birth, see John 1:12-13; Titus 3:5; 1 Peter 1:3, 23; 1 John 2:29; 4:7; 5:1, 4, 18. None of these indicate the need for baptism.

Two, the preposition "of" indicates origin or cause (cp. Gal. 4:4, "made of a woman").

Three, in the Bible "Spirit" can mean God the Holy Spirit, a holy angel, a demon, or the human spirit.

Four, "water" has both literal and figurative meanings in the Bible.

(3) In the light of this information, the following facts relate to this passage.

One, "Spirit" refers to the Holy Spirit (vv. 6-8; Titus 3:5).

Two, since "water" has both literal and figurative meanings, which is the better here? If the literal meaning is intended, then the Lord must be referring to water baptism. But the need of baptism for salvation does not agree with the general teaching of Scripture (Acts 10:43, 16:31; Eph. 2:8-9). We believe that water baptism, as one's formal testimony to his salvational faith, properly follows his salvation (Acts 18:8).

If, as I believe, the figurative meaning of water is intended, then water, according to its biblical usage, can represent several things: spiritual life (John 4:14), the Holy Spirit (7:37-39), the Word of God (Eph. 5:26), or the nations (Rev. 17:1, 15).

(4) The figurative meanings of "water" are the Word of God and the Holy Spirit. Both of these concepts are related to the new birth (John 3:6-8; 1 Peter 1:23). However, which one of these is better in this context? While the Word of God is involved in the new birth, it does not seem, for the sake of consistency, that the Lord would use in this clause a figure of speech for the Scriptures and none for the Holy Spirit. Because of this irregularity and the Lord's statements in the context (6-8), it seems better to interpret "water" as meaning the Holy Spirit who, too, is active in the divine work of regeneration (Titus 3:5) and who is represented in Scripture by water (John 7:37-39).

(5) If, as I believe, "water" refers to the Holy Spirit, then the conjunction "and" introduces an explanation rather than an addition. It explains that water means the Holy Spirit. Thus we understand Jesus to say, "Except a man be born of water, namely, the Spirit, he cannot enter the kingdom of God." This interpretation agrees with the context and with the general teaching of the Scriptures.

4. An Exercise

Following the procedure of Section 2, interpret one of the following verses:

Due Monday Mark 8:34 in the light of Romans 6:1-13. To what does the cross refer?

Mark 12:30 in the light of John 14:15, 31. What does it mean to love God?

James 4:17 in the light of Hebrews 13:21. What does it mean to do good?

Mark 12:30

RULE THREE: *Understand the meaning of the words in the passage.*

---

1. A Description of a Word

A word is a basic unit of language that has meaning. Since words often have more than one meaning, we must consider their various meanings and select the one that best agrees with the passage and its context.

2. The Need for Considering the Meaning of Bible Words.

(1) *Words change in usage over a period of time*.

Gal. 1:6-7

For example, in the King James Version (KJV) we find "let" for "restrain" (2 Thess. 2:7), "prevent" for "go before" (1 Thess. 4:15), "conversation" for "behavior" (1 Tim. 4:12), and "carriage" for "baggage" (1 Sam. 17:22).

(2) *Different words have similar meanings*.

This is especially true in the KJV, for the translators used synonyms rather than the same word repeatedly. For example, various forms of the Greek verb *meno* are translated "abode" (John 1:32), "remaining" (33), "dwelt" (39), "continued" (2:12), "tarry" (4:40), and "endures" (6:27).

(3) *The same word may have different meanings, as determined by its biblical usage and context*.

For example, consider the word "flesh," which has the following biblical meanings:

1) The physical structure of humans and animals (Ex. 29:14; Luke 24:39; 1 Cor. 5:5).
2) Living humans and animals (Gen. 6:17; Acts 2:17).
3) Representing what is human (Eph. 6:5).

4) One's relatives, ancestors, or posterity (Gen. 29:14; Rom. 9:3).

5) Man's weakness and temporariness (Ps. 78:39; Isa. 40:6; Rom. 6:19).

6) Man's responsiveness to God (Ezek. 36:26).

7) Christ's atoning work (John 6:53-56; Eph. 2:15).

8) One's total being (2 Cor. 7:5).

9) Human nature dominated by the sin force[1] (Eph. 2:3, second occurrence of "flesh"). Here the emphasis is on human nature.

10) The sin force dominating human nature (Gal. 5:16; 6:8; Eph. 2:3, first occurrence of "flesh"). Here the emphasis is on the sin force.

(4) *Many words are used both literally and figuratively.*

For an example, the word "cross" has literal meaning in John 19:17 and figurative meaning in 1 Corinthians 1:18, representing our Lord's atoning work.

(5) *Some words, which are also used in sermon and song, often are misunderstood or are not understood.*

Some of these are "forgiveness" (Eph. 1:7), "love" (Matt. 5:44), "soul" (Mark 8:35-36), and "redemption" (Col. 1:14).

3. The Procedure in Applying This Rule

(1) Use a standard English dictionary to learn the ordinary meaning of words that you do not understand.

(2) Learn the meaning of words according to their biblical usage.

1) With the aid of a complete concordance in the Bible version you are using, find the occurrences of the word in the Scriptures. For the KJV, *Young's Analytical Concordance* to the Bible lists the English words according to their Hebrew and Greek roots. This helps us to see their inherent differences.

2) Seek to determine the meaning of this word in the various passages and contexts where it occurs.

---

1. Observe that "sin force" is a better designation than "sin nature" for the energy of sin within us. This agrees with Romans 7:23, 8:2, which calls sin a "law." We essentially have only one nature—the human nature.

1. Eng. meaning
2. Hebrew or Greek def.
3. Conclusion

3) Seek further <u>help from Bible word-study books</u> and Bible dictionaries. (See Appendix D.)

(3) Of the various meanings a word may have in its biblical usage, select the one that <u>best fits</u> the passage being interpreted, <u>its context</u>, and the <u>general teachings</u> of the Scriptures.

4. An Example of This Rule

Consider the word "flesh" in Romans 13:14. "But put ye on the Lord Jesus Christ and make not provision for the flesh to fulfill the lusts thereof."

Following the procedure in Section 3, we have these:

(1) From *Webster's Collegiate Dictionary*: "Flesh": 1, soft part of the body of an animal; 2, edible parts of an animal; 3, a: physical being of man; b, human nature; 4, a: human beings; b, living beings; 5, fleshy plant used as food.

(2) For the various meanings of "flesh" in biblical usage, see Section 2, (3), above. Try these meanings in the place of the word "flesh."

(3) In this context the best choice of meaning for "flesh" in Romans 13:14 seems to be the sin force dominating human nature (Section 2, (3). 10)). Our duty as believers is to submit to Christ and His influence rather than to give ourselves over to sin. This interpretation of "flesh" is in harmony with Romans 6:11-13.

5. An Exercise

By following the procedure in Section 3, learn the biblical usage meanings of one of the following words: heart, spirit, love, sleep, law, or fruit.

RULE FOUR: *Interpret the passage according to its grammatical construction.*

---

1. A Description of Grammar

Grammar is about the relationships of words with other words in the passage to be interpreted. It's also about their structural forms which express these relationships.

The New Intl Dict of New Testa. Theology

Colin Brown

meaning
Form
Function

2. An Overview of English Grammar

As tedious as it may be, take time to review this survey of grammar. An understanding of the grammatical structure of the language, in which the passage we are interpreting is written, is necessary for accurate interpretation. (Model sentences are in parentheses and examples are in bold type.)

(1) The parts of speech

These parts determine the functions of words in a sentence. Consider these parts and their examples.

1) The noun

This is the name of a person, place, thing, or idea. A proper noun is the name of a particular person, place, or thing. (The **man** went to **Chicago**.)

2) The pronoun

This takes the place of a noun or a pronoun. The word which the pronoun replaces is the antecedent. The kinds of pronouns follow:

1. Personal pronoun
   This refers to a person or thing. (The man took a sandwich; and **he** ate **it**.)
2. Possessive pronoun
   This shows possession. (Tom found his book; Jane lost **hers**.) "His" is used here as an adjective, modifying "book."
3. Relative pronoun
   This is used to introduce adjective and noun clauses. They are who, whom, whose, which, and that. (The man, **who** lives next door, became ill.)
4. Interrogative pronoun
   This is used in a question: who, whose, what, whom, which? (**Who** taught the class?)
5. Demonstrative pronoun
   This is used to point out a specific person or thing. They are *this* and its plural form these, *that* and its plural form *those*. (**This** is more helpful than that book.) "That" is used here as an adjective, modifying "book." "This" refers to what is near, "that" to what is remote.

6. Reflexive pronoun
This reflects the action of the verb to the subject. They are myself, yourself, himself, herself, itself, ourselves, yourselves, and themselves. (The boy hurt **himself**.) Ourself is used collectively for myself or ourselves.

7. Indefinite pronoun
This does not refer to a particular person or thing. This includes all, another, any, both, each, either, few, many, more, most, much, none, one, other, several, someone, something, everyone, and everything. (She gave flowers to **everyone**.)

3) *The adjective*   or describes
This modifies a noun or pronoun. It tells what kind (**red** hair), which one (**this** book), or how many (**two** boys).

4) *The adverb*
This modifies a verb, adjective, or another adverb. With verbs it tells how (He ran **quickly**.), when (He arose **early**.), where (The boat went **under**.), or to what extent (The man ran **far**.). Adverbs modify adjectives (She wore a **very** red dress.). They also modify other adverbs (He ran **extremely** far.).

5) *The verb*
This expresses action or helps to make a statement. (Tom, who **is** tall, **painted** the upper part.)

1. Kinds of verbs

(1) Action Verbs
These help to make a statement by expressing action. The kinds of action follow:

1) Transitive action
This directs the action to an object. (The boy **hit** the ball.) "The ball" receives the action "hit."

2) Intransitive action
The action does not require an object to complete the thought. (The eagle **soars**.) Some verbs are used both transitively and intransitively. (We **ate**; they **ate** the pie.)

(2) <u>Linking verbs</u>   *State of being*

These help to make a statement by linking together two words. The most common of these are forms of the verb "be." (The boy **is** tall. The music **sounds** harsh. The flower **smells** sweet.) Many linking verbs may also be used as action verbs. (The mouse **smells** the cheese.)

2. <u>Verb voices</u>

Voice is the relation of the action expressed by the verb to the subject or the form of the verb expressing this relationship. This is either active or passive.

(1) <u>Active voice</u>

The verb expresses the action that is done by the subject. (Helen **drove** the car.)

(2) <u>Passive voice</u>

The verb expresses the action that is done upon the subject. (Hannibal **was driven** by hatred.)

3. Verb <u>tenses</u>

The verb forms show the time of the action or idea that they express.

PRESENT TENSE
(Action occurs at the present time.)

Singular	*Plural*
I sing (talk)	we sing (talk)
you sing (talk)	you sing (talk)
he, she, it sings (talks)	they sing (talk)

PAST TENSE
(Action occurred in the past but did not continue into the present.)

Singular	*Plural*
I sang (talked)	we sang (talked)
you sang (talked)	you sang (talked)
he, she, it sang (talked)	they sang (talked)

FUTURE TENSE
(Action occurs at some time in the future.)

Singular	*Plural*
I shall sing (talk)	we shall sing (talk)
you will sing (talk)	you shall sing (talk)
he, she, it will sing (talk)	they will sing (talk)

PRESENT PERFECT TENSE
(Action occurred at no definite time in the past or it
occurred in the past and is continuing into the present.)

Singular	*Plural*
I have sung (talked)	we have sung (talked)
you have sung (talked)	you have sung (talked)
he, she, it has sung (talked)	they have sung (talked)

PAST PERFECT TENSE
(Action completed in the past before some other past action.)

Singular	*Plural*
I had sung (talked)	we had sung (talked)
you had sung (talked)	you had sung (talked)
he, she, it has sung (talked)	they had sung (talked)

FUTURE PERFECT TENSE
(Action completed in the future before some other future action.)

Singular	*Plural*
I shall have sung (talked)	we shall have sung (talked)
you will have sung (talked)	you will have sung (talked)
he, she, it will have sung (talked)	they will have sung (talked)

6) *The articles*

1. Definite article: the
This indicates a particular noun. (**The** man went
into **the** house.)

2. Indefinite article: a, an
This indicates one of a group or anyone. (**A** man
went into **a** house for **an** hour.) Use "an" before words
beginning with a vowel sound a, e, o, u, and sometimes *y*. Also, use "an" before words beginning with
h when the *h* is silent, as in *hour*.

7) *The preposition*
This shows the relationship of a noun or a pronoun to
some other word in the sentence. It always has some
noun or pronoun for its object. It may consist of one or
more words. (The boy **in** the yard ran **in front of** the car.)
The prepositional phrase, "in the yard," modifies "boy"
like an adjective. He is an in-the-yard kind of boy. "In
front of" modifies "ran" like an adverb. This tells where

he ran. The same word may be either an adverb or a preposition depending on its use in a sentence: as an adverb (The car went **by**.); as a preposition in an adverbial phrase (The car went **by** the house.).

8) *The conjunction*

This joins words or groups of words. There are several kinds of conjunctions.

1. Coordinating conjunctions

These join equal parts of a sentence, such as nouns (The girl has a pencil **and** a tablet.), verbs (The player hit the ball **and** ran.), phrases (The man went into the house **and** up the stairs.), and clauses (The man ate lunch; **and** he went to work.).

2. Correlating conjunctions

These are conjunctions that are used in pairs. (**Neither** a stone **nor** a ball went through the window. **Either** he painted the house **or** he had it sided. **Both** the girls **and** the boys went to the zoo.)

3. Subordinating conjunctions

These conjunctions introduce modifier clauses and noun clauses and make them dependent upon, or subordinate to, the words or clauses to which these clauses are linked.

(1) Introducing modifier clauses

These are adjective and adverb clauses, which modify independent clauses or other dependent clauses. (The car, **that** was in the garage, was destroyed by fire.) This conjunction introduces an adjective clause, modifying "car" and indicating an in-the-garage kind of car. (**When** he went to town, Bob bought a new Dodge.) This conjunction introduces an adverb clause, modifying "bought" and indicating time.

Here is an example that includes both kinds of modifier clauses: (**After** he fished in the river, **which** was north of town, Tom went home.) "After" introduces an adverb clause modifying "went" and indicating time. "Which" introduces an adjective clause modifying river and indicating a north-of-town kind of river.

(2) Introducing noun clauses

These are clauses that function as a noun, such as the subject of a sentence (**That he went to Africa** brought John much publicity.), or as the direct object of such verbs as hearing, telling, feeling, believing, etc. (He heard **that I had returned home**.).

9) *The exclamation*

This expresses an abrupt or emphatic utterance which has no grammatical relation to the rest of the sentence. (**Wow!** What a view!)

(2) The sentence

A sentence is a group of words that contains a subject and a verb and expresses a complete thought.

1) *The parts of a sentence*

1. The subject

This is the part of a sentence about which something is said. (**The man who lives upstairs** gave to the boy the book.)

2. The predicate

This is that part of a sentence which speaks about the subject. (The man who lives upstairs **gave to the boy the book**.)

(1) The verb expresses action or state of being. (The man **gave** to the boy the book.)

(2) The complement completes the meaning begun by the subject and verb. Complements may be nouns, pronouns, and adjectives, but not adverbs.

1) The subject complement follows a linking verb and functions as a noun or an adjective. (Beverly is a **boy**. Beverly is **tall**.)

2) The verb complement receives the action of the verb directly or indirectly. As a direct object (The man gave the **book**.). As an indi-

rect object (The man gave to the **boy** the book.). Observe that the indirect object precedes the direct object and tells to whom or what or for whom or what the action of the verb is done.

When identifying complements, do not mistake them for adverbs. (He went **home**. [an adverb, stating where **he went**] (He bought a **home**. [a direct object])

2) *The kinds of sentences*

1. Declarative sentence
This makes a statement. (**The boy went to school.**)

2. Imperative sentence
This expresses command (**Close the door.**), request (**Give me the food.**), exhortation (**Attend church.**), and the like.

3. Interrogative sentence
This asks a question. (**Who is there?**)

4. Exclamatory sentence
This expresses an abrupt or emphatic utterance, like a strong feeling. (**What a day!**)

(3) The phrase

This is a group of words, without a verb and its subject, that is used as a single part of speech.

1) *Prepositional phrases*

These are groups of words that begin with a preposition and end usually with a noun or a pronoun. These kinds of phrases act like modifiers.

1. The adjective phrase
This modifies a noun or pronoun and usually immediately follows the word it modifies. (The walls **of the room** are dark.) These are room-kind of walls.

2. The adverb phrase
This modifies a verb (The man went **to town.**), an adjective (The man is careful **with his money**.), or an adverb (The delivery man will come later **in the day**.).

2) *Verbals and verbal phrases*

These are verb forms that are used as other parts of speech.

1. The <u>participle</u>   *verbal Adjective*
    This is used as an adjective. (The **moving** car struck a tree.) In the Bible this has the force of a dependent (modifier) adjective clause: The car **which was moving** struck the tree.

2. The <u>gerund</u>   *Verbal noun*
    This is used as a noun. (**Walking** is good exercise.)

3. The <u>infinitive</u>   *Verbal noun   to <u>Verb</u>*
    Usually preceded by "to," this is used as a noun (**To forgive** is often difficult.), an adjective (The mechanic **to call** is Mr. Jones), or an adverb (The plane was ready **to go**.).

3) *<u>Appositive phrase</u>*   *renames the subject*
    This is a noun or pronoun, with its modifiers, which immediately follows another noun to identify or explain it. (Bill, **my brother,** owns the car.)

(4) The clause

This is a group of words that contains a verb and its subject and is used as part of a sentence. To locate the clauses in a passage, look for the verbs and their subjects. There are two kinds of clauses: independent and dependent.

1) *The independent clause*
    This expresses a complete thought and can stand alone. (**The teacher read from the book about Roman history.**) If it has associated dependent clauses, an independent clause is part of the sentence. (**He ate the apple** after he finished his work.) Grammatically, the independent clause is the main clause in the sentence and expresses the main thought of the sentence. Also, the independent clauses in a passage express grammatically the main ideas of the passage.

2) *The dependent clauses*
    These clauses are introduced by a subordinating conjunction, which links them to (1) an independent clause, (2) another dependent clause, or (3) some word in the sentence.

There are two kinds of dependent clauses: modifier clauses and the noun clause.

1. The modifier clause
    This serves as an adjective or adverb.

    1) *The adjective clause* modifies a noun or pronoun. It is introduced by a relative pronoun (who, whom, whose, which, that) and immediately follows the word it modifies. (Thomas Alva Edison was the person **who invented the phonograph**.) This states that he not only was an inventive kind of person but also the inventor of the phonograph.

    2) *The adverb clause* modifies a verb, adjective, or adverb by telling how, when, where, or under what conditions. This clause may stand at any place in the sentence. See the following examples:

    Modifying a verb: (**When we went to Florida**, we left our dog at a kennel.) This clause modifies "left" and indicates the time the dog was left.

    Modifying an adjective: (The room is brighter **since the walls were painted**.) This clause modifies "brighter," showing why the room is brighter.

    Modifying an adverb: (The building burned quickly **because it contained petroleum products**.) This clause modifies "quickly," showing why the building burned rapidly.

2. The noun clause
    This functions as a noun, either as a subject of a verb, its direct object or a predicate nominative: as a subject (**That John went to the Africa was the theme of the report**.); as a direct object (I know **what they said**.); as a predicative nominative (It does not appear **what we shall be**.).

(5) Some common clause conjunctions

These conjunctions link the clauses which they introduce to another part of the sentence and also determine the kind of clauses they are.

1) *Common clause conjunctions*

(See 2 and 3) on the next page for kinds and meanings.)[3]

After (C, 20)
Also (A, 1, 13)
Although (C, 5)
And (A, 1)
As (C, 3, 4, 8, 15, 21)
Because (C, 3)
Before (C, 16, 21)
Besides (A, 1)
But (A, 1, 7, 9, 14)
Consequently (A, 11, 18)
Either—or (B, 19)
Else (A, 6)
Ere (before) (C, 21)
Except (unless) (C, 9, 14)
For (C, 3, 10)
Furthermore (A, 1)
Hence (A, 3)
Henceforth (A, 21
How (C, 3, 4, 6, 15)
If (C, 6, 22; sometimes expresses
   fact ["since"] as in Matthew
   4:3, 6)
Lest (C, 17)
Moreover (A, 1)
Now (Eng. adverb; Gr. *de*, conj.)
   (A, 1; C, 7, 10)
Or (A, 19)
Provided (C, 14)
Save (C, 14)
Since (C, 3, 21)
So (A, 6, 18)

Than (C, 4)
That (C, 3, 12, 17, 18); also a relative pronoun Then (A, 3, 18)
Thence (A, 3, 16, 21)
Thenceforth (A, 21)
Therefore (A, 18)
Though (C, 5)
Thus (A, 18)
Till (until) (C, 21)
Unless (C, 9)
What (that which) (C, 12; has
   force of relative pronoun)
When (C, 21)
Whence (C, 16)
Where (C, 16)
Whereas (C, 7)
Whereby (C, 3)
Wherefore (C, 3)
Wherein (C, 16)
Whereunto (C, 16)
Whereupon (C, 16, 18)
Wherewith (C, 3)
Whether (A, 22)
Which, who, what, that, whom,
   whose, (C, relative pronouns
   introducing adjective clauses;
   12)
While (C, 21)
Whither (C, 16)
Why (C, 3)
Yet (A, 5, 7)

3. These are gleaned from *Standard Handbook of Prepositions, Conjunctions, Relative Pronouns, and Adverbs*, by the Funk & Wagnalls Editorial Staff (New York: Funk & Wagnalls Company, Inc., 1953).

2) *The kinds of clause conjunctions*

A. Coordinative conjunctions
These join equal kinds of clauses. The kind of clause following these conjunctions is determined by the kind of clause that precedes it. (After he ate **and** he bathed, John went to town.) "He bathed" is a dependent clause as is "after he ate."

B. Correlative conjunctions
These are used in pairs. (**Either** he went to town **or** he went to see Tom.) Note: When it is used alone, "either" or "neither" functions as a demonstrative adjective in the sense of "each" or "not each."

C. Subordinative conjunctions
These introduce dependent clauses (modifier and noun clauses).

3) *The meanings of clause conjunctions*

1. Addition, advance
2. Aim, intention, purpose
3. Cause, reason, means
4. Comparison, degree, extent
5. Concession, allowance, acknowledgment
6. Condition
7. Contrast, opposition, adversative
8. Equivalence
9. Exception, exclusion, omission
10. Explanation
11. Inference, conclusion
12. Introducing a noun clause, which functions as the subject or the direct object of the verb of another clause, as something believed, seen, heard, felt, said, etc.
13. Like manner
14. Limitation, exception
15. Manner, method, way
16. Place, position
17. Purpose (aim, end, goal), negative purpose
18. Result, consequence

19. Separation, alternative
20. Sequence in time
21. Time
22. Uncertainty, doubt

Observe again that both prepositional phrases and dependent modifier clauses act like adjectives and adverbs on the words they modify. *Adjectives* modify nouns and pronouns; *adverbs* modify verbs, adjectives, and other adverbs.

Examples: *Adjective*—word (the **red** apple), phrase (the apple **in the bag**), and clause (The apple **that was in the bag** spoiled.).

Adverb—word (He ran **quickly**.), phrase (He ran **into the house**.), and clause (He ran **after the signal was given**.).

3. The Procedure in Applying This Rule

(1) Identify the words in the passage to be interpreted according to their parts of speech see. Section 2, (1).

(2) Recognize the sentences in the passage you are interpreting and identify their kinds (see Section 2, [2], 2).

Since a sentence is a group of words that contains a subject and a verb and that, together with all of its modifiers, expresses a complete thought, first look for the verbs in the passage and their subjects. Keep in mind that a sentence always has (or may be) at least one independent clause. It may also have one or more dependent clauses.

(3) Recognize the clauses in the passage and identify their kinds.

Recognize the clauses by locating the verbs and their subjects. Then identify these clauses and their functions see Sec. 2, (4).

1) The independent clauses (see Section 2, (4), 1))
The independent clauses present the main ideas of the passage. Their order of importance is determined logically by their content or by their position in the passage.

2) The dependent clauses (see Section 2, (4), 2)

These clauses are joined by subordinating conjunctions to independent clauses, another dependent clause, or words in the sentence.

1. The modifier clauses (see Section 2, (4), 2, 1)

Acting like adjectives or adverbs, these clauses modify other words or clauses in the passage. The manner in which they modify these words or clauses is determined by the conjunctions which introduce them and by their positions in the sentence.

2. The noun clauses (see Section 2, (4), 2, 2)

These function as the subject of verbs the predicate nominative or the direct object of certain verbs, such as know, feel, believe, hear, etc.

(4) Identify the conjunctions which introduce the clauses of the passage.

Identify their kind and meaning according to Section 2, (5), 1).

An accurate understanding of these conjunctions is required for an accurate interpretation of the clauses which they introduce. In the case of dependent clauses, an understanding of the subordinate conjunctions is necessary to interpret the impact that these clauses make upon the words or clauses to which they are linked. They show how and with what effect the dependent clauses are linked to the words or clauses that they modify.

When a conjunction has more than one meaning, select the one that best suits the function of the clause and its relation to that to which it is linked and that is in best accord with the teachings of Scripture. Note that in Scripture exposition the dependent clauses often serve as subpoints to the main ideas presented by the independent clauses.

When dealing with a verse or a series of verses in a verse paragraphed edition of the Bible (the format of most KJV Bibles), first recognize the independent clauses in each verse. If the verse is introduced by a conjunction which relates it to the preceding or following verse, then see what the relation of these main ideas, expressed by these independent clauses, is as shown by the meaning of this introductory conjunction.

(5) Recognize and identify the prepositional phrases and the words they modify (see No. 2, (3), 1)).

1) Identify the functions of the prepositional phrases. These phrases function as adjectives or adverbs, depending on the part of speech they modify.

2) Understand the meaning of the prepositions that introduce these phrases (consult a dictionary). If the preposition has more than one meaning, select the one the best suits its function in its relation to the word it modifies, in agreement with the teachings of Scripture.

Observe that the function of prepositional phrases is like that of dependent clauses. Both, in some way, affect the words that they modify.

4. An Example of This Rule

1 Thessalonians 4:13-14

Verse 13: "But I would not have you to be ignorant, brethren, concerning them who are asleep, that you sorrow not, even as others who have no hope."

Verse 14: "For if we believe that Jesus died and arose again, even so them also who sleep in Jesus will God bring with Him."

(1) Identify the parts of speech

Verse 13: "But I would not have you to be ignorant, brethren,
         cnj p rv adv   v pr inf   adj   n
concerning them who are asleep, that you sorrow not, even
  prp   pr cnj v adj   cnj pr   v adv adv
as others who have no hope [sorrow]."
cnj pr   cnj v adj n   (v)

Verse 14: "For if we believe that Jesus died and arose again,
         cnj cnj pr   v   conj n   v cnj   v   adv
even so them also who sleep in Jesus will God bring with Him.
adv adv pr adv cnj v prp n   v   n   v   prp pr

(2) Recognize the sentences.

These verses are one sentence, with one independent clause and several dependent clauses.

(3) Identify the clauses.
    1) The independent clause
Verse 13: "I would not have you to be ignorant, brethren, concerning them who are asleep."
Being the only independent clause in verses 13-17, this clause expresses the main idea of these verses. Introduced by the co-ordinating conjunction "but," this clause indicates a change of direction and an advance in Paul's thought. This clause is declarative.
    2) The dependent clauses

Verse 13: 1. "Who are asleep" (adjective mod. cl.)
            2. "That you sorrow not" (adverb mod. cl.)
            3. "Even as others (sorrow)" (adverb mod. cl.)
            4. "Who have no hope" (adjective mod. cl.)

Verse 14: 5. "If we believe" (adverb mod. cl.)
            6. "That Jesus died and arose again" (noun cl.)
            7. "For even so them will God bring with Him" (adverb mod. cl.)
            8. "Who sleep in Jesus" (adjective mod. cl.)
    (4) Identify the conjunctions which introduce the clauses of the passage (see preceding step).

Verse 13: "But:" coordinative conjunction, stating contrast or exception (cp. v. 9).
        "Who:" subordinative conjunction, relative pronoun introducing an adjective clause.
        "That:" subordinative conjunction, introducing an adverb clause and giving reason.
        "As:" subordinative conjunction, introducing an adverb clause and stating extent.
        "Who:" subordinative conjunction, relative pronoun introducing an adjective clause.

Verse 14: "For:" subordinative conjunction, introducing an adverb clause and giving reason.
        "If:" subordinative conjunction, introducing an adverb clause and stating condition.
        "That:" subordinative conjunction, introducing a noun clause.

"Who:" subordinative conjunction, relative pronoun introducing an adjective clause.

The functions of these dependent clauses follow. See the list above, Sec. 2, (5), 1)):

Verse 13: 1. Introduced by the conjunction "who," this *modifier clause* acts like an *adjective*, for it modifies the pronoun "them." Paul would not have his readers ignorant about their dead friends and relatives. "Sleep" is a euphemism for the state of death.

Verse 13: 2. Introduced by the conjunction "that," this *modifier clause* acts like an *adverb*, for it modifies the verb "have." This clause states the reason for Paul's not wanting his readers to be ignorant.

Verse 13: 3. Introduced by the conjunction "as," this *modifier clause* acts like an *adverb*, for it modifies the verb "sorrow." This clause states the extent to which his readers are not to sorrow. They are not to sorrow as the unsaved do.

Verse 13: 4. Introduced by the conjunction "who," this *modifier clause* acts like an *adjective*, for it modifies the pronoun "others." It identifies "others" as they who have no hope, that is, the unsaved.

Verse 14: 5. Introduced by the conjunction "if," this *modifier clause* acts like an *adverb*, for it modifies the verb "will bring." It states the condition which people must meet if they are to be saved and be reunited with their saved loved ones.

Verse 14: 6. Introduced by the conjunction "that," this *noun clause* is the *direct object* of "believe." It states what must be believed if people are to be saved and go to be with the Lord upon death. See No. 2, (5), 2), 12.

Verse 14: 7. Introduced by the conjunction "for," this *modifier clause* acts like an *adverb*, for it modifies the verb "sorrow" in verse 13. It states the reason why we who are saved should not sorrow as do they who have no hope.

Verse 14: 8. Introduced by the conjunction "who," this *modifier clause* acts like an *adjective*, for it modifies the pronoun "them," the ones who have died and are with the Lord. It identifies those whom the Lord will bring with Him when He comes for the church.

Observe that "but," introducing verse 13, actually introduces the whole passage regarding what Paul wants his readers to know (vv. 13-18) in contrast to what they already knew (vv. 9–12). The "for" that introduces verse 14 actually introduces verses 14-17 and indicates that these verses give the reason for his readers' not sorrowing as others who have no hope.

(5) Identify the prepositional phrases.

Verse 13: 1. "Concerning them," modifying the adjective "ignorant," has *adverb function*. It identifies the people about whom Paul would not have his readers ignorant.

Verse 14: 2. "In Jesus," modifying the verb "sleep," has *adverb function*. It tells us where these people are in their dead condition.

Verse 14: 3. "With Him," modifying the verb "will bring," has *adverb function*. It states the relation of association in which God will bring these people who are now dead.

Observe that the word which a prepositional phrase (or a modifier clause) modifies is recognized as being the one that stands in the closest logical relationship to the phrase. For instance, in verse 13 the phrase, "concerning them," does not modify "have" or "brethren," for the phrases, "have concerning them" and "brethren concerning them," do not have the logical sense that the phrase, "ignorant concerning them," has in this verse.

5. An Exercise

Grammatically analyze John 14:1-3 according to the procedure in Section 3.

RULE FIVE: *Interpret the passage in the light of its background.*

---

1. A Description of the Background

The background of a passage differs from its context. While the context concerns the verses that are before and/or after the passage being interpreted, the background consists of the writer's purpose or reason as well as any <u>historical</u>, <u>geographical</u>, or <u>cultural</u> data that may be in the passage.

2. The Features of the Background

(1) *The writer's <u>purpose</u>, <u>reason</u>, and <u>plan</u>*

Purpose refers to the goal of one's writing, that is, what he wishes to achieve (cp. John 20:31; 2 Cor. 2:1-3). Reason refers to the motivation or justification for writing (Prov. 1:1-7). Both of these may be stated, as seen in the previous examples, or implied (cp. 1 Cor. 1:10; 5:1; 6:1; 9; 7:1; 8:1; 11:2; 15:12; 16:1).

Both purpose and reason must be distinguished from the writer's *plan*, which gives the primary outline of his literary work (see Rule One, Section 2). His plan is shown by the main ideas of his literary work while his purpose and reason are stated or implied by his assertions or by his appeals to his readers.

(2) *Historical data*

This concerns the persons, nations, events, and dates that are found in the passage.

For example, Herod's destroying the infants of Bethlehem (Matt. 2:16) is better understood when we know that he previously had members of his own family put to death in order to preserve his rule from rivals.

(3) *Geographical data*

This is about place names and other geographical features that are found in a passage.

For instance, it is stated in Acts 16:12 that Philippi was a colony. Whey they arrived in this city, Paul and his associates did not find a synagogue there. This was probably due to the city's being a military center rather than a commercial one like Thessalonica, which was more attractive to commercially minded Jews.

(4) *Cultural data*

This concerns the customs, social relations, way of life, religion, and productivity of the people to whom the passage relates.

For example, the Lord declared that the gates of Hades would not prevail against the Church (Matt. 16:18). The word "gates" in this verse represents the place authority. In biblical times, the gate of a town was the place where the local elders met to hear the complaints of the people and to decide civil matters (Ruth 4:1-2). The elders sat at the gate, for this was where the townspeople passed on their way to and from their agricultural and pastoral fields. With this background in view, we understand the Lord to say that the Church, unlike pre-cross believers, will never come under the authority of Hades, the place where Old Testament people went when they died. Today, all who are saved go directly to Heaven to be with the Lord when they die (2 Cor. 5:6, 8).

We must distinguish between the cultural custom of which a passage may speak and the trans-cultural biblical principle that this custom may illustrate. For instance, Paul directed his readers to greet one another with a "holy kiss" (1 Thess. 5:26), a custom that is still practiced in many places. The question is this: Should we practice this in our churches? While the cultural means of expressing Christian love varies, such as shaking hands or hugging, the principle remains that we are to love one another (John 13:34-35). The practice of the holy kiss is cultural; Christian love, however it is expressed, is trans-cultural. It is a biblical principle that all believers are to observe.

3. The Sources of Background Information[4]

How do we gain this background information? By . . .

(1) Becoming acquainted with the historical passages in the Bible.

(2) Referring to source books about the persons and events of biblical times. These sources include Bible encyclopedias, dictionaries, histories, and biographies.

(3) Consulting atlases and maps of Bible lands and books about the nations that existed during the periods of Bible history.

(4) Consulting special introductions to the Old and New Testaments. These deal with the authorship, purpose, plan, and date of each of these Testaments.

(5) Referring to books on biblical customs and manners.

(6) Reading commentaries on the passage being interpreted.

(7) Considering the notes and comments given in study Bibles.

---

4. See the list of titles in Appendix D.

4. The Procedure in Applying This Rule

Seek answers to the following questions:

(1) What is the author's purpose for writing? His reason? What is the plan of his literary work?
(2) Is there any historical data in the passage being interpreted or in its context?
(3) Is there any geographical data in the passage or in its context?
(4) Is there any cultural data in the passage or in its context? Does this cultural data express any trans-cultural biblical principle that we should observe today?

5. An Example of This Rule

Using 1 Corinthians 11:2-16 as an example, here are answers to the questions of Section 4.

Question 1: Regarding the writer's reason, it appears that this passage is a part of the major division wherein Paul deals with disorders relating to public worship (11:2—14:40). These disorders include those relating to the veiling of women (11:2-16), the Lord's supper (11:17-34), and the exercise of spiritual gifts (12:1—14:40).

Question 2: Regarding historical data, there is none in this passage except a reference to the creation of man (9).

Question 3: There is no geographical data in this passage. Corinth was the capital of the Roman province of Achaia (southern Greece). Being a commercial center as well as a colony, it had a mixed population. The church consisted largely of Gentile Greek converts.

Question 4: Women praying and prophesying with covered heads (and their neglect of this custom) was a cultural matter (5-6).

Should this custom be observed today? One, if this was wholly cultural, then it is no longer binding on us. Two, if this custom is wholly trans-cultural, then we should observe it in our churches. And three, if its purpose is to illustrate a biblical principle, then we see in this practice of covering the head a sign of the woman's submission to the man (7-9).

Actually, the principle of female submission is trans-cultural (Gen. 3:16; Eph. 5:22-24) while the means of signifying this submission is cultural, governed by the customs of various peoples.

6. An Exercise

Following the procedure in Section 4, gather background information and evaluate its impact upon the meaning of one of these passages:

1 Kings 12:29-30; 13:1-3. Why was this altar a threat to Judah?

John 13:4-6. Why did Peter refuse to allow the Lord to wash his feet?

John 8:48. Why did the Jews call Jesus a Samaritan when they knew that He was Jewish?

Genesis 23:7-11. Why did Abraham have to purchase the field when he bargained for the cave? (Note that the KJV word "give" in this chapter means "sell.")

RULE SIX: *Recognize, identify, and interpret any figurative expression in the passage.*

We should strive to interpret the Bible literally according to the normal usage of its words. However, a literal interpretation of a passage of Scripture recognizes any figurative expression that may be present and seeks to understand the literal truth that this conveys.

1. A Description of a Figurative Expression

A figurative expression is a word, phrase, or clause that is used to convey meaning other than that which is literal, or natural, to it.

For an example, Jesus described false prophets to be "ravening wolves" (Matt. 7:15). It would be absurd to think that false prophets are real wolves.

How does one recognize a figurative expression? A word, phrase, or clause should be regarded as a figurative expression when its literal, usual meaning is unsuitable or absurd in its context or is in conflict with the general teachings of the Bible.

Historical, Gramatical, Contextual, Literal Interpretation.

2. The ~~Purposes~~ Reasons for Figurative Expressions

Why did God include figurative expressions in the Bible when they often seem to hinder our understanding of the Word? Here are two answers.

(1) *Figurative expressions convey truth much more vividly and powerfully than literal words do.* normal MATTER of fact words do

For instance, in Proverbs 15:3 we read, "The eyes of the LORD are in every place, beholding the evil and the good." This statement is much more vivid than the declaration that the LORD is omniscient, or that He is aware of everything.

those who reject God's word

(2) *Figurative expressions conceal truth from ~~the unsaved~~ (Matt. 13:10-15) as well as convey truth to the saved (16).* MT 12:38-39

Relates to parables

The presentation of truth in an unclear manner was God's response to the unsaved who suppressed divine revelation in unrighteousness (Rom. 1:18; see Matt. 11:20-24; 12:14, 24, 38-39). Since the Holy Spirit is our Teacher, figurative speech is not a barrier. Actually, it stimulates the study and interpretation of the Word.

3. Some Kinds of Figures of Speech

The following list gives the more common figures of speech that are found in the Bible. Examples of figurative expressions are in bold type.

(1) *Simile*

This is an expressed comparison.

John wrote of the Lord Jesus, "His head and His hairs were white **like wool**" (Rev. 1:14). Ordinarily, "like" is a preposition and "as" is a conjunction. "As" is commonly used in the KJV as a preposition. Today, "as" is sometimes used as a preposition to denote closer equivalence than "like." In the KJV "like unto" also expresses comparison.

(2) *Metaphor*

This is an implied comparison. Notice that the prepositions of comparison (like, as) are omitted. Also, observe that metaphorical phrases and clauses are called idioms.

Hypocatastasis - Direct naming of something

Ps 22

The Lord Jesus said, "You are the salt of the earth" (Matt. 5:13).

(3) *Symbol*

This is similar to a *metaphor*. While a metaphor always has figurative meaning, a *symbol* has both literal and figurative meanings at the same time. Symbols are always things; they are never people. People and events are represented by Old Testament types or New Testament parables, as we shall see later.

Jesus said, "This **cup** is the new testament (covenant) in My blood, which is shed for you" (Luke. 22:20). Our Lord was referring to an actual cup (and its contents) as well as to what the cup represented, namely, His blood that ratified the New Covenant and that was shed for His people.

Also, the tabernacle, with its furnishings and ritual, provides many symbols relating to Christ and His priestly work (Ex. 25—40). (See Appendix B for other symbols.)

(4) *Idiom*

This is a metaphorical phrase or clause that has other than literal meaning and that is approved by common usage.

Paul wrote, "The spirit that now worketh in the **children of disobedience** . . . and were by nature the **children of wrath**" (Eph. 2:2-3). To be the child of something means to have its qualities. Unsaved people are characterized by disobedience toward God and by being the objects of divine anger.

(5) *Synecdoche*

One, this is a word for a part of something and that represents the whole entity of which it is a part. For instance, if someone said that he had bought a new set of wheels, this could mean a new car. In this case, the word "wheels" is a synecdoche that represents the car.

Two, a synecdoche can also be a word for the whole of something and that represents a part of the entity of which it is the whole. For instance, if someone said that he ate an orange, this would normally mean that he ate the edible part, not the rind and seeds, too. In this case, the word orange is a synecdoche that represents what was eaten.

In the Bible, synecdoches that represent the whole of

something are much more common than those that represent a part of the whole. Study the following examples:

1) A part standing for the whole of something Luke recorded, "We were in all in the ship two hundred three-score and sixteen **souls**" (Acts 27:37). Since the soul is a part of human nature, "<u>souls</u>" stands for people.

Paul wrote, "Being now justified by His **blood**" (Rom. 5:9). "Blood" stands for our Lord's atonement since His dealing with our sins required both His death and the shedding of His blood. See verse 10, "We were reconciled to God by the **death** of His Son." "Death" also stands for His atonement.

James wrote, "But every man is tempted when he is drawn away of his own **lust** and enticed" (Jas. 1:14). "Lust" stands for the sin-force within us, with its enticement for us to yield to its demands and to sin (cp. Rom. 13:14; Gal. 5:16).

Paul declared, "God . . . commands all men everywhere to **repent**" (Acts 17:30). "Repent" stands for salvational faith, which consists of one's assent to the facts of the gospel, repentance, and trust in Jesus and His atoning work.

2) The whole of something standing for its part

Paul wrote, "And so **all Israel** shall be saved" (Rom. 11:26). "All Israel" stands for the elect of Israel, the true Israel, or the Jewish remnant, that shall be saved (2:28-29; 9:6). Obviously, it does not stand for the political nation or for all the Jews.

In Ecclesiastes 11:1 we read, "Cast thy **bread** upon the waters, for thou shalt find it in many days." "Bread" is a synecdoche for the seed-grain that was sown, germinated, matured, was ground into flour, and was made into bread.

(6) *Metonymy*

This is the word that stands in a close relation to something, but unlike a synecdoche it is not an actual part of what it represents. For instance, a policeman's badge represents the authority of the municipality, but it is not a part of that authority.

Paul wrote, "For the preaching of the **cross** is to them that perish foolishness" (1 Cor. 1:18). "Cross" represents our Lord's atoning work. As an instrument of execution, the cross had no part in the atonement, but it was closely related to this because the Lord Jesus died upon it.

Jacob prophesied, "The **scepter** shall not depart from Judah" (Gen. 49:10). A "scepter" represents regal authority, but it is not a part of this authority.

John wrote, "To them that believe on His **name**" (John 1:12). "Name" represents our Lord's atoning work. It s not a part of this work, but it represents Him and His work.

The LORD said, "At the **mouth** of two witnesses . . . shall the matter be established" (Deut. 19:15). "Mouth" represents testimony, but it is not a part of this testimony, which consists of words.

(7) *Hyperbole*

This is a deliberate exaggeration made for emphasis.

Jesus said, "And if thy right eye offend thee, **pluck it out** . . . and if thy right hand offend thee, **cut it off**" (Matt. 5:29-30). The Lord is not directing His people to dismember themselves. In the light of Romans 6:1-13 and Colossians 3:5, we are to deal radically with sin by refusing to submit ourselves to it for its evil expressions. We are to reckon ourselves to be dead to this evil force and to be alive unto God; and we are to act accordingly (Rom. 6:11-13).

(8) *Rhetorical Question*

This is a question that has only one, obvious answer, which is not (and need not be) expressed.

Jesus asked His enemies, "**Which of you shall have an ass or an ox fallen into a pit and will not straightway pull him out on the sabbath day?**" (Luke 14:5). The answer, though not given, is obvious.

(9) *Irony*

This says the opposite of what the speaker means. It is usually indicated by the tone of voice.

Paul wrote, "**Now ye are full, now ye are rich, ye have reigned as kings without us**" (1 Cor. 4:8). The reader will recognize this figure of speech and determine its tone from the context. Also, see 2 Corinthians 11:4.

(10) *Sarcasm*

A cutting remark that, in this case, shows the vanity of its hearer's pretension or hypocrisy.   *I KINGS 18:27*

Jesus said to His enemies, **"Woe unto you, scribes and Pharisees, hypocrites! For ye devour widows' houses and for a pretence make a long prayer"** (Matt. 23:14). Unlike irony, sarcasm occurs in a context of hostility. Our Lord's righteous indignation is expressed here toward His enemies.

In 1 Corinthians 4:8, I believe that Paul uses irony, for he is writing with loving concern for his people at Corinth, who were being misled by false teachers.

(11) *Euphemism*   *I Cor 11:30*

This substitutes a more agreeable expression for something that is unpleasant, distasteful, or painful.

It is said of Joseph regarding Mary, "And [he] **knew** her not till she had brought forth her firstborn son" (Matt. 1:25). "Knew" represents his having sexual relations with her.

Paul wrote, "Them also who **sleep** in Jesus will God bring with Him" (1 Thess. 4:14). "Sleep" represents the state of death of Christians.

(12) *Litotes*

This is the denial of a thing in order to express its opposite. "He that makes haste to be rich **shall not be innocent**" (Prov. 28:20). He will not be without guilt if this is his life's ambition.

(13) *Pleonasm*

This is excessive or repeated words which are used for emphasis.

Paul wrote, "Bless them who persecute you; **bless,** and curse not" (Rom. 12:14).

(14) *Ellipsis*   *I Jn 2:18-19*

This is an omission of words needed to complete a thought or sentence. These words, missing in the original language manuscripts, are often supplied by translators in italics.

Paul wrote, "Now then we are ambassadors for Christ, as though God did beseech **you** by us; we pray you in Christ's stead, be ye reconciled to God" (2 Cor. 5:20). Since the Corinthian believers were reconciled to God through salvation, "men" would be a better substitute than "you."

The Lord Jesus said, "Abide in Me, and I (**will abide**) in you" (John 15:4). As we abide in Him, He promises to abide in us in the full productivity of His life and power.

(15) *Personification*

This is speaking about nonpersonal things as though they are persons.

The psalmist wrote, "Let the floods **clap their hands**; let the hills **be joyful together**" (Ps. 98:8).

(16) *Anthropomorphism*   *a form of man*

This is any human part, action, or characteristic that is attributed to God.

The LORD said, "Your new moons and your appointed feasts my **soul** hateth" (Isa. 1:14). Essentially, God does not have a soul, as we do. Being spirit, His nature has no parts.

(17) *Anthropopathism*

This is any human emotion or feeling that is attributed to God.

The LORD said, "I am **weary** to bear them" (Isa. 1:14). "For I the LORD thy God am a **jealous** God" (Ex. 20:5). God's jealousy is based on His claim to the exclusive devotion of His people. He is zealous to maintain the purity of their love for Him.

(18) *Zoomorphism*

This is any animal part, action, or characteristic that is attributed to God.

The psalmist wrote of God, "He shall cover thee with His **feathers**, and under His **wings** shalt thou trust" (Ps. 91:4). God's protection and care are described as being like that of a bird for its young.

4. Some Observations About Figurative Expressions

(1) We must have a clear conception of the thing on which

the figure is based or from which it is borrowed. This especially applies to interpreting similes, metaphors, symbols, idioms, anthropomorphisms, and the like.

For instance, John wrote of Jesus, as seen in a vision, "Out of His mouth went a sharp **two-edged sword**" (Rev. 1:16). This was a Roman sword, twenty to twenty-four inches long, with both edges sharpened.

(2) We must discover the leading idea conveyed by the figurative expression. The context or other passages where the figure is found will show what this emphasis should be.

For one example, the meaning of "sword" in Revelation 1:16 is Jesus' words, as shown in Isaiah 11:4 and 2 Thessalonians 2:8.

(3) Observe that in the case where the figurative expression suggests several meanings or functions for its leading idea, its context determines the right meaning or function.

For instance, "A sharp two-edged sword" conveys the functions of a weapon or a cutting and piercing instrument, and the meanings of warfare, destruction, judgment, authority, and the like. In the context of Revelation 1:16 (10-20), a cutting and piercing instrument seems to be the best function conveyed by this sword since Jesus' words work in this manner in the hearts of His people.

(4) While they are not to be taken literally, figurative expressions convey literal, actual truth that God wants His people to understand.

For instance, in Revelation 1:16 the Lord's words, vividly portrayed as a piercing and cutting sword, are seen as judging His people's inmost thoughts and attitudes (Heb. 4:12) and as exerting a sanctifying influence on their lives (John 15:3; 17:17). They sanctify by exposing and cutting away the hindering corruption in their lives.

5. The Procedure in Applying This Rule

(1) Recognize any figurative expression in the passage.

We recognize a word, phrase, or clause as a figurative expression when its literal meaning does not make sense, indicates an absurdity, or contradicts the general teachings of the Bible. The examples, given in Section 3 above, will help you to recognize these.

(2) Upon recognizing the figurative expression, identify its figure of speech by the kinds and examples given in Section 3.

(3) Reflect upon the various ideas that belong to the figurative expression, especially if it is a simile, metaphor, or symbol, and select the one that best suits the context, as in Section 4 (1) and (2).

(4) Give the meaning of the figurative expression.

> 1) Do this according to its kind of figure (Sec. 3) and to the inherent ideas that the figurative expression suggests (Section 5, (3)).

> 2) Look for the interpretation of the figurative expression in its context. With the aid of a concordance of the version of the Bible you are using, look for other passages where the figurative expression occurs and see if the interpretation is given in these passages or in their contexts.

> 3) Seek to interpret the figurative expression in harmony with its context and the general teachings of the Scripture.

> 4) Write out your interpretation of the figurative expression.

(5) Read the passage with your interpretation of the figurative expression in order to see how your understanding harmonizes with the passage and its context and what it contributes to the context.

6. An Example of This Rule

Romans 12:1

"I beseech you therefore, brethren, by the mercies of God, that ye present your bodies a living sacrifice, holy, acceptable unto God, which is your reasonable service."

Following the procedure of Section 5 with Romans 12:1, I offer this:

(1) This verse has two figurative expressions: "bodies" and

Gen. 42:38

Ps 8:3-4

"sacrifice." Are we to present only our bodies to the Lord? Usually a sacrifice consists of a slain animal. To my mind, these words, taken literally, do not make sense. They must be figurative expressions.

(2) Regarding their kinds of figures of speech, "bodies" is a synecdoche and "sacrifice" is a metaphor.

(3) Regarding the ideas that these figurative expressions convey, "bodies" are the physical bodies of Paul's Christian readers. The ideas associated with "sacrifice" are atonement, worship, and cost.

(4) Regarding the meaning of these figurative expressions, "bodies" is a synecdoche for the total person. In Ephesians 5:23 the husband is described as the savior (protector) of his wife, who is represented by the word "body." Paul seems to refer to himself by "body" in Philippians 1:20. The ability of the tongue to defile the "whole body" (James 3:6) seems to refer to its defiling one's total person. Thus in Romans 12:1 Paul is exhorting his Christian readers to give their total selves wholly to God.

"A sacrifice" is a metaphor, which states an implied comparison. It tells what this presentation is to be like. "Sacrifice" reminds us of the Levitical offerings under the Mosaic Law (Lev. chapters. 1—5). In the case of Romans 12:1, however, the sacrifice is living rather than dead.

The ideas associated with offering sacrifices are atonement, worship, and cost. With the Lord Jesus' being our substitute, the idea of atonement is ruled out here. On the other hand, the ideas of worship and cost remain. Our giving ourselves to God for ministry is an act of worship. Also, it is to give Him our most precious possession. In view of the fact that the Lord Jesus readily gave Himself for us, we cannot do less for Him and His cause than to give Him our total being. Moreover, we are to do His will, as revealed in the following chapters, while we still have life and strength to do so. (See 2 Sam. 24:24; 2 Cor. 5:14-15.)

Our offering ourselves to God is one of several spiritual sacrifices that we as spiritual priests are to make unto God (1 Peter 2:5; Heb. 13:15-16; Rom. 15:16; Phil. 2:17).

(5) With this interpretation of these figurative expressions,

I understand Paul to say, "I beseech you, brethren, . . . that you present your total selves, a living, costly offering . . . unto God."

7. An Exercise

Following the procedure of Section 5, recognize, identify, and interpret the figurative expression(s) in one of the following passages: John 1:29; 2 Timothy 2:21; Jeremiah 23:29; Genesis 42:38; James 4:1; Ephesians 4:13; and Psalm 8:3-4.

RULE SEVEN: *Recognize and interpret any type in the passage.*

---

1. A Description of a Type

A type is an Old Testament person, event, or thing that illustrates some New Testament truth.

For example, Adam is a type of Christ (Rom. 5:14-21; 1 Cor. 15:44-49). Also, the rock in the wilderness is a type of Christ (Ex. 17:6; 1 Cor. 10:4).

2. Some Observations About Types

(1) Unlike symbols, types include people and historical events as well as things.

(2) The New Testament person, event, or thing that the type portrays is called the anti-type.

(3) While many types in some way portray the Lord Jesus Christ, not all are about Him.

For example, Hagar portrays the Mosaic Law which represents the principle of human works, while Sarah portrays the New Covenant which represents the principle of God's grace (Gal. 4:19-31). These principles are methods by which God deals with people.

(4) Some hold that types are only those people, events, and things of which the New Testament speaks as being types (see the examples in Section 1). To my mind, anyone or anything in the Old Testament which strikingly portrays some New Testament truth may be understood typically as well as literally. However, the natural, or literal, interpretation of the record of these people, events, and things should always have first consideration.

① There must be a _natural_ connection between Anti type & Type

② The Person, thing or event in the O.T. must have been real

(5) The recognition, interpretation, and application of types create greater interest in the Old Testament and make it more useful. (See 1 Cor. 10:11; Rom. 15:4.)

3. The Procedure in Applying This Rule

(1) Recognize the type, if any, in the passage.

When interpreting an Old Testament passage, especially a historical narrative, be alert for people, events, or things that clearly illustrate New Testament truth. (For a list of types see Appendix C.)

(2) Identify the anti-type New Testament truth that the type portrays.

With the aid of cross-references or a concordance, see if and how the type is interpreted in the New Testament.

(3) List the features of the type that illustrate those of the anti-type, the New Testament truth that the type portrays.

As with similes, metaphors, and symbols, one must have a true conception of the type upon which the anti-type is based. Also, one must carefully observe what the context tells about the type and its relation to the narrative.

Do not invent parallels for the details of the type that are not clearly reflected by the anti-type. Avoid establishing a teaching upon a type, for types serve to illustrate truth already established by the New Testament. For example, some people say that the Church will not be on earth during the Tribulation Age because God preserved Noah from the flood. They believe that the ark, with its occupants, is a type of the Church. In response, we grant that the ark may illustrate this truth, but it should not be used to establish, or prove, it.

4. An Example of This Rule

Following the procedure given in Section 3, let us see how the passover lamb is a type of Christ, God's Lamb who took away the sins of the world (Ex. 12:3-13; John 1:29).

(1) The type is the lamb that God directed Israel to slay and eat on the night when the death angel passed over the land of Egypt. ③ A Type must have devine design
④ Avoid building a teaching on a type
⑤ The Anti Type is greater to the type.
⑥ A type will have a predictive

Also, God directed Israel to apply the lamb's blood to the door posts of their homes. See Exodus 12:3-13.

(2) The Lord Jesus Christ is the anti-type, as seen in John 1:29, 36; Acts 8:32; 1 Peter 1:19; and Revelation 5:5-14.

(3) Observe the following parallels, from features found in Exodus 12:3-13:

> 1) The lamb was to be without blemish (v. 5; see 1 Peter 1:19; 2:22; 1 John 3:5). The Lord Jesus was sinless.
>
> 2) The lamb was observed for a time (v. 6; see Luke 2:52; 3:23).
> The Lord Jesus lived almost thirty years in the sight of the people of Nazareth.
>
> 3) The lamb was slain by the Israelites (v. 6; see Acts 3:12-15).
> It was Israel's intention to kill Jesus, but He voluntarily laid down His life (John 10:17-18).
>
> 4) The lamb's blood was shed and applied (v. 7; see Eph. 1:7).
> The value of Jesus' atoning sacrifice, represented by His blood, is divinely applied to one's account when he trusts Him as Savior.
>
> 5) The lamb's flesh was eaten (v. 8; see John 6:53). The Lord's words are a hyperbole, expressing the need for personal appropriation of His atoning work by faith.
>
> 6) The lamb's flesh was roasted, not boiled (v. 8; see Isa. 53:10). The fire speaks of God's wrath, which Jesus received for our sins (Heb. 12:29; Isa. 53:10).
>
> 7) That part of the lamb's carcass which was not eaten was wholly consumed by fire; it was not allowed to spoil (v. 10; see Acts 2:22-27). After His death our Lord's body did not experience corruption.

5. An Exercise

Following the procedure in Section 3, interpret the type found in one of the following passages: Deuteronomy 18:18; Genesis 4:1-5; or 2 Samuel 9.

RULE EIGHT: *Recognize and interpret any parable or allegory in the passage.*

---

1. The Descriptions of Parables and Allegories

(1) A parable is a statement or brief story, taken from daily life, which portrays some spiritual truth.

(2) An allegory is an extended metaphor, by which some spiritual truth is illustrated. Unlike a parable, an allegory does not tell a story.

2. The Purposes for Parables and Allegories

Most of the biblical parables and allegories were told by the Lord Jesus. (For a list of these see Appendix A.) His purposes for using these are given in Matthew 13:10-17.   Mark 4:10-11

(1) To withhold truth from them who were unreceptive to His teaching (vv. 11-15).

Jesus' speaking in parables was a divine judgment on those who rejected His clear preaching and teaching (cp. John 10:1-6; see Matt. 11:20; 12:22-24, 34, 38-42). The disciples were surprised when Jesus used this manner of teaching, for this had not been His custom (Matt. 13:10).

(2) To convey truth to them who were receptive to His teaching (vv. 16-17).

Our Lord also used parables and allegories to convey to His people truth in an impressive way. It is easier to understand and retain truth given in story form than by unqualified statement. Remember that the Holy Spirit teaches His people divine truth, even when it is packaged in parables. But the world does not have access to His teaching ministry (John 14:17).

3. Two Observations about Parables and Allegories

(1) Both parables and allegories are interpreted by the same procedure.

(2) It is important to distinguish between what parables and allegories teach and what they illustrate.

Parables and allegories were given to teach specific truth. On the other hand, many parables and allegories have features which illustrate truth which was not the speaker's intention to convey. The interpreter must find what truth the speaker intended to teach by his parable or allegory.

4. The Procedure in Applying This Rule

When interpreting parables and allegories, seek answers to the following questions:

(1) To whom and about what had the speaker been talking? (See the context.)

(2) What prompted the giving of the parable or allegory? (See the context.)

(3) To whom was the parable or allegory addressed? (See the context.)

(4) What are the natural, true-to-life features of the parable or allegory?

(5) What data do parallel passages, elsewhere in the Bible, add to your understanding of the parable or allegory?

(6) Did the speaker give an explanation of any features of the parable or allegory?

(7) What central truth or duty does the parable or allegory teach?

The central truth is set forth by the main features of the parable or allegory and by what is said about these features. Avoid making every minor detail of the parable or allegory symbolical of truth.

(8) How did the teaching of the parable or allegory apply to the one(s) to whom it was given? (See the context.)

(9) What application of this teaching can be made to yourself or to others to whom you minister?

(10) In addition to what the parable or allegory teaches, does

it illustrate any biblical truth other than what the speaker intended to convey?

If you should use the parable for illustrating truth, make this known to your hearers. They should know that your use of the parable was not the purpose for its being originally given.

(11) If the parable or allegory was given by Jesus, what does it teach about Him?

5. An Example of Interpreting Parables

The Parable of the Good Samaritan (Luke 10:30-35; context, vv. 25-37).

Following the procedure of Section 4, we give answers to the interpretative questions about this parable.

Question 1: This parable arose out of a conversation that Jesus had with a certain expert in Jewish law about the reception of eternal life (vv. 25-28).

Question 2: Jesus told the parable in response to the lawyer's question about the identity of his neighbor (v. 29). Earlier, the lawyer had asked Jesus what he should do to inherit eternal life. (Note that he did not ask how to be saved.) In response, the Lord referred the man to what the Law of Moses said about this (vv. 26-28; Deut. 6:5; Lev. 19:18; 18:5). Loving God and neighbor was the Jews' foremost duty. Knowing that he did not keep this aspect of the law, the lawyer tried to justify himself by asking who was his neighbor. Jesus answered his question by this parable.

Question 3: This parable was addressed to the lawyer.

Question 4: Going from Jerusalem to Jericho, a man fell among robbers, who beat him, stripped him, and left him for dead. A Jewish priest and a Levite, fearing ritual contamination, passed by the victim without assisting him. But a Samaritan merchant, who by Jewish values was a nobody, personally ministered to the man and paid others to care for him.

Question 5: This is the only record of this parable.

Question 6:   Jesus does not give any explanation of the para-
              ble. He does ask the lawyer who was neighbor
              to the victim (v. 36).

Question 7:   By this parable Jesus teaches that one's neighbor
              is any person who has some need to which he
              can minister, even at personal cost.

Question 8:   This parable answered the man's question (v.
              29). That he understood this answer is indicat-
              ed in verses 36-37.

Question 9:   Within the range of our opportunities and re-
              sources, we who are saved have the duty of
              ministering to all who have need. This is an
              expression of Christian love (1 John 3:16-18;
              Gal. 6:10; 1 Tim. 6:17-18).

Question 10:   This parable clearly illustrates salvation. The
              victim portrays the unsaved person, spiritually
              dead and in debt for his sins. The priest and the
              Levite represent the Law of Moses or any system
              of human works, which is powerless to save.
              Rejected by the Jews, the Samaritan depicts the
              Lord Jesus, who came to us and paid the price
              of redemption.

Question 11:   The parable illustrates Jesus' infinite love and
              grace in His saving us from our sins when we
              were helpless to help ourselves (Rom. 5:6).

6. An Example of Interpreting Allegories

The Allegory of the Vine and the Branches (John 15:1-6;
context, 13:31—16:33)

Following the procedure of Section 4, we give answers to the
interpretative questions about this allegory.

Question 1:   This allegory was spoken by Jesus to His apostles
              on the eve of His death. He was speaking about
              the earthly life and ministry of His people during
              His absence from them. See John 13:33; 14:12—
              16:33.

Question 2:   This allegory was prompted by the fact that in a
              few days these men would be serving as the

Lord's representatives and would be introducing Christianity to the world.

Question 3: This allegory is addressed to the Lord's people (John 13:33).

Question 4: The features of the allegory are the vine, branch, and vinedresser, and the part each has in the production of fruit.

Question 5: There are no parallel passages. Other references, such as Galatians 5:22-23; Colossians 1:10; Romans 1:13, indicate the nature of the fruit we are to bear.

Question 6: Jesus identified Himself to be the True Vine, His people to be the branches, and God the Father to be the Vinedresser (1-3).

Question 7: By this allegory the Lord Jesus taught that the production of spiritual fruit is accomplished by the cooperative effort of the Vine, the branch, and the Vinedresser. The Lord Jesus, the Vine, produces the fruit in the lives of His people. The duty of His people, the Branches, is to abide in Him, which allows Him to produce this fruit in their lives. The duty of God the Father, the Vinedresser, is to remove the unfruitful branches and to prune the fruitful ones.

Question 8: The allegory shows that it is the duty of the Lord's people to abide in Him and to submit to those means that the Father uses to prune their lives, namely, His Word (v. 3) and His discipline (Heb. 12:11). Our abiding in the Lord, which allows Him to abide in us and to produce this fruit in our lives, appears to include our being submissive to Him, our obeying Him, our trusting Him, and our communicating with Him. See Matthew 11:28-30; Galatians 2:20; 1 Corinthians 1:9; Colossians 3:16; and Philippians 4:13.

Question 9: The same as that of Question 8. Apart from Jesus, we cannot be fruitful or do anything that pleases Him (John 15:5; cp. Phil. 4:13).

Question 10: None that I can see.

Question 11:   This allegory shows that the Lord Jesus is the
new life (eternal life) of His people as well as its
expression in their daily lives. It also reminds
us of our responsibility to the Father's dealings
with us and our accountability to Jesus as His
servants (John 15:2, 6; cp. Heb. 12:5-11; 2 Cor. 5:
10).

7. An Exercise

Select one of the parables or allegories from the list in Appendix A; and interpret it by following the procedure in Section 4 above.

RULE NINE: *Recognize and interpret any dispensational feature in the passage.*

---

1. Some Descriptions

(1) *A dispensation*

A dispensation is the responsibility, or stewardship, that God gives to certain people for a time.

In Paul's case, his personal responsibility of ministry is described as a stewardship (Eph. 3:2).

The major divine dispensations follow:

A. The Dispensation of Created Man [*Innocence*] (Gen. 1:28-29; 2:15-17)

B. The Dispensation of Fallen Man (Gen. 3:16—4:7)

C. The Dispensation of Governed Man (Gen. 9:1-7)

D. The Dispensation of the Patriarchs (Gen. 12:1; 17:1; 26:5; 31:3, 13; 35:1; 46:1-4)   *Promise*

E. The Dispensation of the Mosaic Law (Ex. 20:1-7; 21:1-23; 23:14-19; Lev. 1—27; Num. chapters. 5, 6, 9, 10, 27—30) *613 laws O*

F. The Dispensation of Grace [*or The church*] (Titus 2:11-12; most of the commands of the New Testament) *≤30 rules to follow in N.T.*

G. The Dispensation of Christ's Earthly Rule (Isa. 2:1-3)

Some will add an 8th — Tribulation Period

(2) *Dispensationalism*

This is the interpretation and application of the Bible that recognizes the various dispensations and their features, the people to whom each dispensation is given, and the portion of the Bible that relates to these people.

For example, the law of Moses was given to Israel. The portions of the Bible that relate to these people living under this law are Exodus ch. 19 through Malachi ch. 4, also, Matthew through John.

(3) *An age*

In the Bible the word "age" has several meanings. In addition to being a span of human life or of years, an age has two special meanings, both of which are determined by their contexts:

1) **Dynamically,** an age is a period of time that is characterized by some activity of God, man, or Satan.

The period during which the Lord Jesus is building His Church is called **the Church Age**. According to the pretribulation rapture view, the period immediately after the rapture of the Church and before Christ's second coming to earth is called **the Tribulation Age** because of the many judgments earth dwellers will experience during this time (Rev. 6—19). The period during which God deals with Israel (the seventy-sevens of Daniel 9) is sometimes called **the Jewish Age** (cp. Matt. 24:3). Our Lord's reign over the earth for a thousand years is called **the Kingdom Age**.

2) **Ethically,** an age is what the world is morally and philosophically at any moment of its history.

Paul wrote, "And be not conformed to this world [age]" (Rom. 12:2). The apostle was urging his Christian readers not to adopt the sinful lifestyle and thinking of the unsaved. Also, Ephesians 2:2, "world."

(4) *A covenant*

This is a solemn statement that God made to certain people of what He promised to do.

While a dispensation states in the form of command what God wants people to do, a covenant declares in the form of promise what He will do.

The major divine covenants follow:

A. The Noachic Covenant (Gen. 9:8-17)

B. The Abrahamic Covenant (Gen. 17:1-19; 12:1-3; 13:14-17; 15:4-21; 22:15-18)

C. The Mosaic Covenant (Ex. 19:1-8; 24:1-8; Lev. 18:5)

D. The Palestinian Covenant (Deut. 28:1—29:1; 30:1-10)

E. The Davidic Covenant (2 Sam. 7:10-16)

F. The New Covenant (Jer. 31:31-40; Heb. 8:6-13; 10:15-17; 12:24).

Being offered to all people, the New Covenant promises salvation to all who trust Christ and His atoning work.

I have not found any biblical evidence for the Covenants of Works and of Grace, as covenant theology holds, or for the Edenic Covenant, as many dispensationalists hold. It is very likely that, when He clothed Adam and Eve with the skins of animals, God spoke to them about salvation, which anticipated the coming and the atoning work of the Redeemer (Gen. 3:21). By this action He established the Old Testament means of atoning for human sins and laid the basis for a duty of the following four dispensations— the offering of animal sacrifices when approaching God.

2. Some Observations

(1) Most of the commands of the New Testament comprise the Dispensation of Grace which Christians are to follow today.

This portion of the Bible was given by the Lord Jesus for the direction of His people (John 16:12-15; Eph. 4:21; Col. 3:16; Gal. 6:2; Rev. 1:1-2).

(2) While our Lord's teaching, preserved in the Gospels, was directed to people living under the Mosaic Law, still many of

these people were His disciples who would be living and ministering in the Dispensation of Grace.

Most of what Jesus taught related to the lives of these people in the new dispensation. His teaching that was related to the Mosaic Law, such as the Sermon on the Mount (Matt. 5—7), contained truth that applies to us today. Being absolute, God's moral requirements are the same for any dispensation.

(3) We must recognize that, while it is all profitable to us (2 Tim. 3:16; Rom. 15:4; 1 Cor. 10:11), the Bible is not all about us.

Most of the Old Testament concerns God's dealings with Israel under the Mosaic Law. Since the New Testament gives the Lord's dispensation for His people today, we may follow the instructions of the Old Testament insofar as they reflect, or are in harmony with, those of the New Testament.

For instance, we do not follow the sacrificial ritual given in Leviticus, for this was a part of the Dispensation of the Mosaic Law given to Israel. The New Testament does not direct us to offer this kind of sacrifices since the Lord Jesus has made His once-for-all sacrifice for us. On the other hand, we read in Psalms, Proverbs, and Ecclesiastes of the duty of fearing God, which is also given us in the New Testament (Ps. 34:9; Prov. 1:7; Eccl. 12:13; Eph. 5:21; 1 Peter 2:17).

(4) There are prophetic passages in the New Testament which, I believe, do not directly apply to us today (Matt. 24—25; Rev. 6—18).

These will be of special value to God's people who will be living in the Tribulation Age.

(5) There are recorded in Acts certain events, experiences, and practices that belong to the transition into the Dispensation of Grace and that are not normative for us today.

These include waiting for the promise of the Father (1:4), the experience of the Pentecostal phenomena (2:1-4), the common holding of private property (2:45), and praying for the gift of the Holy Spirit (8:14-17). Today, we receive the Holy Spirit's indwelling, baptism, and anointing at salvation. It is not necessary to seek these as additional works, or blessings, of grace.

(6) Dispensationalism insists on a literal interpretation of biblical prophecy.

Literal interpretation of prophecy was established by the literal fulfillment of those prophecies that related to our Lord's first coming to earth. Still, dispensationalism recognizes the figurative expressions that are found in the prophetic passages and seeks to understand the literal truth they convey. Growing out of this literal interpretation of prophecy is the recognition of the distinction between the nation of Israel and the Church, as separate entities in God's program for His redeemed people (cp. 1 Cor. 10:32).

(7) While the blessings of salvation (the forgiveness of sins, the reception of eternal life, and a personal relation with God) are the same for all of the redeemed, dispensationalists believe that various groups of God's people have different duties and serve different functions.

For example, Israel had the Mosaic Law and functioned as the LORD's wife (Hosea 2). On the other hand, the Church has the New Testament and functions as Christ's espoused bride (Eph. 5:25-32; 2 Cor. 11:2). During our Lord's earthly kingdom, Israel will have an earthly political entity and inheritance (Ezek. 36:24-28). The Church, not having these earthly features, will be with Christ (1 Thess. 4:17).

(8) An age should not be equated with a dispensation although it may, or may not, run concurrently with a dispensation.

An age emphasizes a divine activity while a dispensation emphasizes a divine requirement. Regarding their coexistence, it appears that the Dispensation of Grace covers both the Church Age and the Tribulation Age since there is no prediction of a new dispensation being given during this time of worldwide trouble. It is the stewardship that all saved people will observe during these times. On the other hand, the Jewish Age (the 490 years of Daniel 9), is included in the Dispensations of the Mosaic Law and of Grace (the Tribulation Age).

(9) Dispensationalists recognize the divine covenants and the people to whom they are given.

Rather than being various expressions of one covenant (the Covenant of Grace, as covenant theology holds), I believe that these are separate covenants, given to specific peoples. Except for the Noachic covenant which was made with humans and animals (Gen. 9:8-17), the other divine covenants relate in some way to Israel. The promises of the New Covenant, a salvational covenant, are fulfilled to all Jews and Gentiles who receive the Savior.

(10) This ninth rule of interpretation largely concerns the application of the Scripture to be interpreted.

It asks, To what dispensation does the passage belong and to what people does it apply? While all Scripture is profitable for our learning and sanctification (2 Tim. 3:16-17; cp. Rom. 15:4; 1 Cor. 10:11), still not all biblical commands relate to all people. These commands, belonging to distinct dispensations, apply only to the people to whom the dispensations are given.

3. The Procedure in Applying the Rule

Seek answers to the following questions:

(1) To what dispensational section of the Scriptures does the passage to be interpreted belong?

This is recognized by the time span of the dispensation, during which it is in force, and by the Scripture that falls within this span. For instance, all of the Old Testament falls within the Dispensation of the Mosaic Law, except Genesis 1:1 through Exodus 18:27. Also, the four Gospels fall within this dispensation. Acts through Revelation 3 falls within the Dispensation of Grace.

(2) To what dynamic age, if any, does the passage belong?

For instance, the New Testament epistles belong to the Church Age since they were written to and about people who lived during this time. Matthew 24—25 and Revelation 4—19 describe events that belong to the Tribulation Age.

(3) Does the passage address itself to some dispensational duty for the people to whom it belongs or to some event of the age to which it belongs?

(4) While belonging to a section of Scripture that lies within the span of a certain dispensation or age, does the passage give duties or contain information about people or events relating to another dispensation or age?

Prophecy serves as an example here. Prophetic statements written in one dispensation or age may refer to events in another dispensation or age. For example, the prophecy of Isaiah 11:1-9, given in the Dispensation of the Mosaic Law, speaks about features belonging to the Dispensation of Christ's Earthly Rule. Again, Revelation 4—19, written during the Church Age, refers to events that will occur during the Tribulation Age. Also, the Olivet Discourse (Matt. 24—25), given in the Dispensation of the Mosaic Law, gives instruction for the elect remnant of Israel who will be living during the Tribulation Age, in the Dispensation of Grace.

(5) If the passage does not lie within the scope of the Dispensation of Grace or the Church Age, does it give duty or illustrate truth that can be applied to us today?

To apply to us, this duty must correspond to the requirements of the Dispensation of Grace, that is, the duties of the New Testament. For example, nine of the Ten Commandments (except Sabbath-keeping; Ex. 20:3-17) are found in the teachings of the Dispensation of Grace (Rom. 13:8-10; Eph. 4:28-29; 6:1-2; Col. 3:5; 1 Thess. 4:3.7; James 5:12; 1 John 3:11-15; 5:21).

(6) Is there any reference in the passage to one of the divine covenants?

If so, what covenant is mentioned, what covenant promise is referred to, and to whom was it given?

4. An Example of This Rule

The Sermon on the Mount (Matt. 5—7), given by Jesus during His Galilean Ministry.

Following the procedure of Section 3, we give answers to the interpretative questions about this passage.

Question 1:   This passage belongs to that span of time covered by the Dispensation of the Mosaic Law. In

Question 2:   fact, much in our Lord's address alludes to this law.

Question 2:   The sermon belongs to the Jewish Age, the period of 490 years during which God is dealing with Israel, according to the prophecy of Daniel 9.

Question 3:   The Lord Jesus shows that acceptable law-keeping (obedience to God) involves right attitudes and motivations as well as outward conformity to God's requirements (5:19-48). See the answer to Question 5.

Question 4:   There is very little prophecy in this sermon. References appear to be made to the coming millennial kingdom (5:5) and to the judgment of the nations when the Lord will determine who are qualified to enter His kingdom (7:21-23; cp. 25:31-33).

Question 5:   Since most of the sermon was addressed to the Lord's disciples who would be living in the Dispensation of Grace (5:3—7:12), its teachings apply to us as well, in spite of its allusions to the Mosaic Law.

These allusions are mostly to the ethical teachings of the law that are repeated in the Dispensation of Grace. By-passing the ceremonial aspects of the law and Sabbath-keeping, the Lord emphasizes godly character (5:3-12), holy function (5:13-16), and right doing (5:17—7: 12).

Further, He emphasizes the life of true righteousness as this concerns God's will (5:17-48), religious observances (6:1-18), worldliness (6:19-34), and social relations (7:1-12). The Lord also makes an appeal to the lost (7:13-27).

This sermon is beneficial, not only to us who live in the Church Age but also to them who will be living in the Tribulation Age and the Kingdom Age. Some hold that this sermon belongs exclusively to the Kingdom Age, but this does not appear to be so since Jesus spoke of conditions, such as persecution, that will not exist at that time (5:11).

Question 6:   No reference is made to any divine covenant.

5. An Exercise

Recognize and apply any dispensational features in Genesis chapters 1 and 2.

RULE TEN: *Recognize and interpret any prophetic feature in the passage.*

---

1. Descriptions of Prophecy

(1) In the strictest, biblical sense, prophecy is any communication from God by words through an inspired person (cp. Deut. 18:18; Heb. 1:1-2; 2 Peter 1:21).

(2) This tenth rule concerns prophecy in its popular sense any prediction or vision about the future beyond the time of its being given.

2. Some Observations About Prophecy

(1) There are two basic methods of interpreting prophecy.

> 1) *The allegorical method*
> This method subjectively regards the words of the prophecy to have other, hidden meaning than what they say. This allows unrestricted speculation and denies the objective testing of the interpretation. Needless to say, this method is to be avoided.

> 2) *The literal method*
> This method grants to each word of the prophecy the meaning it ordinarily has in normal, biblical usage. As objectively as possible, it seeks to interpret the prophecy literally. This method allows the self-consistency of Scripture (see Rule Two, 1) and the teachings of the Bible to control the interpretation.

(2) The literal method of interpreting prophecy (which I favor) recognizes figurative expressions and seeks to understand the literal truth they convey.

(3) Many biblical prophecies are related to the two comings of the Lord Jesus to earth and to the events that are associated with these comings. In the New Testament some prophecy is

also related to the return of Christ for His Church (1 Thess. 4:13-17; 2 Thess. 2:1).

(4) Dispensationalism favors a literal interpretation of prophecy.

This view is supported by the literal fulfillment of those prophecies relating to our Lord's first coming. Moreover, by the literal method of the interpretation of prophecy, one sees a future restoration of the nation of Israel to their land, a distinction between the redeemed nation of Israel and the universal Church of Christ, an earthly millennial rule of Christ, several resurrection events, and several judgment events.[4]

(5) Regarding the time of the fulfillment of prophecy

1) Some Old Testament prophecies were fulfilled in the Old Testament period. For example, Israel's deliverance from Egypt (Gen. 15:13-14 with Ex. 12:31-41).

2) Other Old Testament prophecies were fulfilled in the New Testament period. For example, Jesus' incarnation and His ministry to Israel as the Messiah (Isa. 7:14; 61:1-2*a* with Luke 4:16-21).

3) Some New Testament prophecies were fulfilled in the New Testament period. For example, the start of the Church on the Day of Pentecost (Matt. 16:18 with Acts 1:5; 11:15-18).

4) Many prophecies of both Testaments remain to be fulfilled in the future. For example, the Lord's millennial, earthly rule (Isa. 11:1-9; Rev. 20:4-6).

3. The Procedure in Applying This Rule

(1) Identify the prophetic portion, if any, in the passage to be interpreted.

This is recognized by its containing a theme of Bible prophecy and/or by its having verbs with future tense. For example, see Deuteronomy 30:1-10.

---

4. See F. H. Barackman, *Practical Christian Theology*, "Eschatology."

(2) Distinguish between the historical or contemporary events given in the passage and the future events that are predicted.

(3) Recognize, identify, and interpret any figurative expression that may be found in the passage.

Bible prophecy often has figurative expressions, either in the context or elsewhere in the Bible.

(4) Study other biblical passages that refer to the prophecy of the passage. Also, consider what the Bible as a whole teaches about this prophetic theme.

(5) As objectively as possible, interpret the prophecy literally, in harmony with its context and the general teachings of Scripture.

(6) When the prophecy allows more than one interpretation, choose the one that best fits the context and that presents the fewest interpretative problems.

(7) Consider the possibility of multiple fulfillments of the prophecy. Identify these, if any, and determine what is the final fulfillment.

Prefulfillments are partial; the final fulfillment is complete. For instance, in Joel 1:1—2:11 the locust plague portrayed an invasion of Judah from the north (2:20). This had prefulfillment in the Babylonian invasion some 200 years later. Its final fulfillment will be in the Tribulation Age as indicated by the reference to the Day of the LORD (1:15; 2:1, 11) and by other features in its context.

(8) Seek to learn why the prophecy was given as well as what it means. (See the context.)

(9) Seek to learn by whom and to whom the prophecy was given. (See the context.)

(10) Seek to learn what the prophecy contributes to its context as well as to the biblical teaching of this theme.

(11) Determine if and how the prophecy relates to the Lord Jesus and to His first or second coming to earth or to His coming for the Church. The Church was not a subject of Old Testament prophecy.

4. An Example of This Rule

Following the interpretative directions of Section 3, we give the data that we gleaned about Isaiah 7:14.

(1) The prophecy is this: "Behold, a virgin shall conceive and shall bear a son, and shall call his name Immanuel."

(2) The context (vv. 1-6; also, see 2 Kings 16) reveals that a coalition of Israel and Syria threatened Judah. Ahaz, king of Judah, refused to ask the LORD for a sign that would assure him of God's protection (vv. 10-12). Therefore, God gave the sign of a virgin's bearing a son.

(3) There are no figurative expressions in the verse. However, the child's name is significant. It means "God with us."

(4) This prophecy is quoted in Matthew 1:23. We know from the New Testament that when He came to earth, God the Son took upon Himself a human nature, divinely conceived in the virgin Mary (Luke 1:26-38).

(5) The prophecy simply states that a virgin woman will conceive, give birth to a son, and will call his name Immanuel. At first glance, nothing is unusual about this, except the name of her son. This, together with the quotation in Matthew 1:23, shows that it refers to Jesus.

It is noteworthy that the usual Hebrew word for virgin (*bethulah*) is not used here; but the Greek word for virgin (*parthenos*) is used in Matthew 1:23. The Hebrew word for young woman (*almah*), employed here, is always used in the Old Testament of a virgin (cp. Gen. 24:43).

(6) This prophecy has only one interpretation.

(7) This prophecy seems to have a prefulfillment in the birth of Isaiah's son (Isa. 7:15-16; 8:3-4, 18).

(8) This prophecy was given as a sign to Ahaz and Judah to assure them that they would not be destroyed by the threatening coalition of Israel and Syria (see v. 16).

(9) From the context we learn that this prophecy was given to the house of David (vv. 12-13) by the LORD (v. 10). Ahaz belonged to this house.

(10) The prophecy was the sign by which the LORD assured Ahaz of Judah's survival. In fact, Judah was still in existence some 700 years later when the prophecy was fulfilled. Moreover, it gave us another name of the Lord Jesus, "Immanuel," meaning "God with us."

(11) This prophecy related to the Lord Jesus' first coming to earth.

5. An Exercise

Interpret the prophecy in Micah 5:2 or in John 14:1-3, according to the procedure in Section 3.

RULE ELEVEN: *Recognize, identify, and interpret any doctrinal words in the passage.*

---

1. A Description of Doctrinal Words

Doctrine concerns teaching. Doctrinal words are those biblical words that represent, or relate to, the teachings of the Bible.

2. Some Observations About Doctrine and Doctrinal Words

(1) Doctrinal words, which usually are nouns, verbs, and verb forms, can be recognized by their relation to the teachings found in the Bible.

(2) There are passages in the Bible that deal with a doctrine without using the actual doctrinal word. For instance, in Romans 8:28-30 Paul is speaking about salvation, from its beginning in God's purpose to its completion in the believer's glorification. Yet, the word "salvation" does not occur in this passage. However, terms like "justified" that relate to salvation do occur.

(3) There are doctrines which are taught in the Bible for which there are no technical biblical designations to represent them.

Examples of these are the doctrines of the Trinity and of eternal security. Neither "Trinity" nor "eternal security" occur in Scripture.

(4) The major doctrines of the Scriptures, which are represented and taught by doctrinal words, are the Bible, God, God the Father, the Lord Jesus Christ, God the Holy Spirit, Angels,

Bibliology
Theology

Man, Sin, Salvation, the Church, the Christian Life, and Future Prophetic Events.

For instance, "redemption" relates to Salvation, "Comforter" to God the Holy Spirit, "the body of Christ" to the Church, and "grace" to God, being one of His attributes.

Many doctrinal words relate to more than one Bible teaching, such as "forgiveness" to Sin and Salvation, and "faith" to Salvation and the Christian Life.

(5) The understanding of a Bible doctrine is based on the plain statements of Scripture rather than on obscure or figurative ones, such as types or parables. Also, this understanding must be based upon all the passages that refer to the doctrine rather than on a selected few.

(6) We must use caution when formulating doctrine by inference, that is, by conclusions that are not clearly stated in the Scriptures but that are derived from biblical truth. This is a valid practice, but it must always be subject to and tested by the general teachings of Scripture.

An example is infant salvation. Based on the truths that Christ died for all humans, that salvation is by divine grace, and that God is just, it may be assumed that people who die in infancy are at death graciously delivered from the effects of original sin and are taken to be with the Lord.

(7) To become acquainted with the major doctrines of the Bible, one will receive help from any sound, standard book on Bible doctrine or systematic theology.[5] Again, all doctrinal helps must be evaluated in the light of the Scriptures.

3. The Procedure in Applying This Rule

(1) Recognize the doctrinal words that may be in the passage to be interpreted.

(2) Look for any expressions of doctrinal concepts in the passage where their usual doctrinal words are missing or for which no special words occur in the Bible.

(3) Identify the specific doctrines to which these words or concepts are related.

---

5. Barackman, F. H., *Practical Christian Theology.*

(4) Observe how these words or concepts are related to these doctrines according to the general teachings of the Scriptures.

(5) Consider how other passages in the Bible support or modify these doctrinal words or concepts.

(6) Observe what these words or concepts in the passage being interpreted say about these doctrines.

(7) Notice what these words or concepts add to the biblical teaching of these doctrines.

(8) Summarize the doctrinal teachings of the passage.

4. An Example of This Rule

Following the procedure in Section 3, let us look at Philippians 4:19: "But my God shall supply all your need according to His riches in glory by Christ Jesus."

(1) The doctrinal words
   "God," "shall supply," "need," "glory," and "Christ Jesus."

(2) The doctrinal concepts
   None are indicated.

(3) Their specific doctrines
   "God" relates to God.
   In context "shall supply" relates to God.
   In context "need" relates to Christian Life.
   "Glory" relates to God.
   "Christ Jesus" relates to the Lord Jesus Christ.

(4) The relation of these words or concepts to their doctrines
   "God" is the generic name of Deity in the Bible.
   "Shall supply" relates to God's care of His people.
   "Need" speaks of the lack we Christians experience in daily life. In context, it seems to refer to temporal need.
   "Glory" relates to God's nature. "Jesus" is the human name of God the Son.
   "Christ" is a human title, indicating a function or office.

(5) The teaching of other passages
   "God"—This is the most common name of Deity in the Bible (cp. Gen. 1:1).

"Shall supply"—That God cares for His people is a blessed truth (Ps. 37:23-29). However, in 2 Corinthians 8:1-5; 9:6-7, Paul teaches that God provides generously for those who themselves are generous and who give by His grace. The Philippian church was one of Paul's supporting churches.

God is aware of the needs of His people and will provide for these when we are walking His fellowship and blessing (Ps. 103:13-14; Matt. 6:31-33; John 7:37-39).

"Glory"—The glory of God is any manifestation of the qualities of His nature, such as His power and wisdom, displayed by His works (Ps. 19:1).

"Jesus Christ"—"Jesus" is the personal, human name given to the Lord eight days after His birth (Luke 2:21). It means "The Lord is salvation" (Matt. 1:21).

The title "Christ" means "Anointed One," referring to Jesus' divine appointment to be the Father's Servant (Isa. 42:1; Phil. 2:7) and to His enablement by the power of the Holy Spirit (Isa. 61:1; Acts 10:38).

(6) What these words or concepts say about these doctrines.

This passage states that God cares for His people, that He is rich in glory, and that He provides through the Lord Jesus.

(7) What these words or concepts contribute to biblical teaching.

Paul asserts the magnitude of God's provision by comparing this with the riches of divine glory, which are infinite.

(8) Summary

Paul assures his generous readers (Phil. 4: 14, 18) that his God will provide for their temporal needs, in keeping with the wealth of His infinite glory and through the intermediate agency of Christ Jesus. Although the Philippians had given sacrificially, the apostle assures them that God will more than make it up to them. God is generous toward those who are generous toward His people.

5. An Exercise

Using the procedure of Section 3, recognize, identify, and interpret the doctrinal words in John 3:16.

5

Interpretation and Organization

Having gathered the interpretative data from the procedures of Rules One through Eleven in Chapter 4, how are we to utilize and organize this material? Here are some suggestions.

1. The Summary of the Interpretative Data

(1) As you work through Rules One through Eleven, make written notes of the information that you obtain from following the interpretative procedural steps.

(2) When you have finished gathering this analytical data, make a chart for each verse (see chart A, on page 89).

> 1) At the top of the page, write out the verse as given in the Bible.
>
> 2) In a column on the left of the page, list the interpretative rules. Then enter to the right of each rule a summary of the information that you obtained from following the procedural steps of each rule. If there is no information, such as prophetic data, then write "None" in the space for Prophecy (Rule Ten).
>
> 3) At the foot of the page give the interpretation by rewriting the verse in your own words in expanded form.

Verse: ....

Rules:
Context	: ....
Whole Bible	: ....
Words	: ....
Grammar	: ....
Background	: ....
Figurative Example	: ....
Type	: ....
Parable/Allegory	: ....
Dispensation	: ....
Prophecy	: ....
Doctrines	: ....

Interpretation: ....

Chart A

Repeat this summary procedure for each verse in the passage being interpreted.

2. The Organization of the Passage

Having summarized the interpretative data of each verse, then make an outline of the passage according to its grammatical-topical organization, as follows:

(1) Look for the main ideas, or topics, as expressed by the independent clauses.

(2) Recognize the relationships between these independent clauses.

The conjunctions, if any, that introduce these independent clauses reveal their structural relationships. Their content indicate their logical relationships. These relationships show how the leading ideas of the passage fit together.

(3) Observe how these main ideas, expressed by the independent clauses, are modified by their subordinate dependent clauses. (See Rule Four, 3, (3) pp. 39ff., and 4, (3) p. 46.)

(4) Write an outline of the structure of the passage, showing the main ideas and their supporting thoughts. (See Rule One, 2, (2).)

> Here is an outline of John 15:1-6; the theme is "fruit-bearing."

A. Jesus' Declaration (1) (Ind. cl.)
B. His Explanation (vv. 2-6)
   There is no conjunction; a logical relationship.
   - a. The Father's Part in Fruit-bearing (vv. 2-3)
     - (a) He removes the unfruitful branches (2*a*) (Ind cl)
     - (b) He prunes the fruitful ones (2*b*-3)
       - a) Statement (2*b*) (Ind. cl.)
       - b) Reason (2*c*) (Dep. cl., 3rd "that")
       - c) Means (3) (Dep. cl., "now" explanation)
   - b. Jesus' Part and Our Part in Fruit-bearing (vv. 4-6)
     - (a) His command (4)
       - a) Statement (4*a*) (Ind cl)
       - b) Reason (4*b*) (Ind. cl. modified by dep. cl.)
         A logical relationship.
     - (b) His promise (5-6)
       - a) Assertion (5*a*) (Ind. cl.)
       - b) Statement (5*b*) (Ind. cl.)
       - c) Reasons (5*c*-6)
         - a. Impossibility (5*c*) (Dep. cl., "for")
         - b. Loss (6) (Ind. cl. modified by dep. cl.)
           A logical relationship.

Observe that the main parts of the outline, expressing the main ideas of the passage, are independent clauses. See A; B, a, (a); B, a, (b), a); B, b, (a), a); and B, b, (b), a) and b).

3. The Rewriting of the Passage

When you have summarized the analytical data of each verse and have produced the grammatical-topical organization of the passage, briefly give your understanding of the passage by rewriting it in your own words according to its essential organization. As much as possible, avoid using the same words that are in the passage, especially the nouns, verbs, and clause conjunctions. Also, avoid using more words than necessary and expressing ideas that are not indicated in the passage. Show the relationships of the main ideas by expressing the meaning of the connecting words (conjunctions, see pp. 36ff.).

More detailed interpretation will be preserved in your written notes of the interpretative rules and their procedures. Be certain that your interpretation is in agreement with the passage's context and the general teachings of the Scriptures. These are the only means that you have to verify the accuracy of your interpretation. Depend upon the Holy Spirit to teach and guide you in your study.

4. The Contribution of the Passage

Consider how the interpreted passage contributes to the theme of the context and to the biblical teachings to which it refers.

6

The Personal Application
of the Scriptures

Gaining insight into the meaning of Scripture should never be an end in itself. We should always make some application of God's Word to our life (Deut. 29:29; Ps. 1:1-3; 2 Tim. 3:15-17). Here are some suggestions.

1. Use the Bible in regular fellowship with God (Ps. 1:1-3)

Since the Bible is God's Word, we allow Him to speak to us by reading it and meditating upon what He says. God speaks to us by bringing to our attention some word or phrase, which stands out above the rest.

2. Look for truth that will relate to your personal need (Ps. 119:105)

Whatever your need, one way by which God ministers to us is through the Scriptures. He does this by His words of encouragement, instruction, command, rebuke, warning, guidance, and assurance. When we read the Word with our needs in mind, we shall find something that will be helpful.

A chief means of help is His promises. God's great promises assure us what He will do in response to our faith. They also provide a basis for our faith in Him. Make a list of biblical promises and the needs to which they apply. Refer to this list when needs arise in your life and rest upon the suitable promises that relate to your needs. This allows God to minister to you during these times of need.

3. Be a doer of the Word (James 1:22-25)

God teaches us and ministers to us by His Word only so far as we suitably respond to Him (Luke 8:18). Our acting upon His Word in the Lord's strength not only allows Him to work in our lives but also prepares the way for further understanding of His truth.

4. Prepare to give an answer to your faith (1 Peter 3:15)

From the Bible we learn not only what we should believe but also why we should believe it. Only the Bible gives the answers to the great philosophical questions with which men have wrestled through the ages. As believers, we must be prepared to give the biblical view regarding origin, purpose, meaning, relation, and destination as well as to bear witness to the uniqueness of the Christian faith. When people ask us why be believe there is a God, Christianity is the true religion, and Jesus is the only Savior, we must be ready to give them a biblical reply.

5. Develop a biblical ethical code (Ps. 119:9-11)

Only God by His Word provides the absolute standard for our behavior that is right and pleasing to Him. By commands and principles, the New Testament sets forth the kind of life that we Christians are to live. In these days of moral relativity and permissiveness, we need to pursue that moral life-style which conforms to God's Word. We are called unto holiness (1 Thess. 4:3, 7; 1 Peter 1:15).

6. Build a fund of biblical teachings (1 Tim. 4:13)

When you learn new truth, relate it to what you already know about the matter. Aim to understand what the Bible teaches about its great doctrines and to share this truth with others. This fund of doctrine not only will edify you but it will also guard you against false doctrine, which abounds today.

7. Prepare to minister to others (2 Tim. 2:2)

Ever keep in mind that God ministers to the spiritual needs of people through His Word (2 Tim. 3:15-17). He ministers to us in our real life situations through His Word so that we, in turn, can minister to others in their need. It is not God's design for us to keep His truth locked up within ourselves. We have the good news of salvation in Jesus to give to others. We also have the other teachings of His Word, with their many applications to life, to share as well.

The Word of God is profitable for teaching us, reproving our wrongdoing, showing us how to get right with God, instructing us in the will of God, and preparing us for every good work (2 Tim. 3:16-17).

"Let the word of Christ dwell in you richly" (Col. 3:16).

7

A Summary of This Interpretative Method

The following is a summary of this method of Bible interpretation, including the interpretative procedures that have been given in the preceding pages. When you interpret a passage of Scripture, follow the steps of this summary. Consult the appropriate pages for information about and illustration of these steps.

1. **Adjustment and Prayer to the Holy Spirit**
2. **Analyses of the Passage to Be Interpreted**

    (1) *Contextual analysis* (Rule One)   Vs 27+28   Imed.

    1) What is the <u>immediate</u> context of the passage to be interpreted and its theme?

    2) What is the larger context of the passage to be interpreted and its theme?

    3) Who is writing and/or speaking?

    4) Who is being addressed?

    5) What does the context contribute to the passage being interpreted?

    6) What does the passage being interpreted say in the light of its context?

93

7) What does the passage being interpreted contribute to the context and to its theme?

(2) *Biblical Analysis* (Rule Two)   The Lords supper

1) After studying the passage in its context, list the truths, or topics, of the passage as they are expressed by key words and ideas.

2) See how these topics, expressed by their key words and ideas, occur elsewhere in the Bible and what additional information these passages give about these topics.

3) In the light of the information you have gathered in your research, decide what facts particularly relate to the topics expressed in the passage being interpreted.

4) In the case of more than one biblical interpretation, select the one that best fits the topic and its context.

5) Consider the understanding that this selected biblical data gives to the topics in the passage.

(3) *Word analysis* (Rule Three)

1) Use a standard English dictionary to learn the ordinary meaning of words that you do not understand.

2) Learn the meaning of words according to their biblical usage.

3) Of the various meanings a word may have in its biblical usage, select the one that best fits the passage being interpreted, its context, and the general teachings of the Scriptures.

(4) *Grammatical analysis* (Rule Four)

1) Identify the words in the passage to be interpreted according to their parts of speech (see Section 2, (1) pp. 31f.).   Just the word unworthly (a one sentence statement

2) Recognize the sentences in the passage and identify their kinds (see Section 2, (2), 2) p. 38).

3) Recognize the clauses in the passage and identify their kinds (see Section 2, (4) pp. 39f.).

4) Identify the conjunctions that introduce the clauses of the passage (see Section 2, (5) pp. 40f.).   with the exception of and

5) Recognize and identify the prepositional phrases and the words they modify (see Section 2, (3) pp. 38f.).

Vs 27-28

(5) *Background analysis* (Rule Five)

   1) What is the author's purpose and/or reason for writing? What is the plan of his book?
   2) Is there any historical data in the passage being interpreted or in its context?
   3) Is there any geographical data in the passage or in its context?
   4) Is there any cultural data in the passage or in its context? Does this cultural data express any trans-cultural biblical principle that we should observe today?

(6) *Figurative expression analysis* (Rule Six)

   1) Recognize any figurative expression, if any, in the passage being interpreted.
   2) Upon recognizing the figurative expression, identify its figure of speech.
   3) Reflect upon the various ideas that belong to the figurative expression and select the one that best suits the text and its context.
   4) Give the meaning of the figurative expression.
   5) Read the passage with your interpretation of the figurative expression to see how your understanding harmonizes with the passage and its context and what it contributes to the context.

(7) *Typical analysis* (Rule Seven)

   1) Recognize the Old Testament type, if any, in the passage.
   2) Identify the New Testament anti-type.
   3) List the features of the type that illustrate those of the anti-type.

(8) *Parabolic analysis* (Rule Eight) *Does not apply*

   1) To whom and about what had the speaker been talking?
   2) What prompted the giving of the parable or allegory?
   3) To whom was the parable or allegory addressed?
   4) What are the natural, true-to-life features of the parable or allegory?

5) What data do parallel passages, elsewhere in the Bible, add to your understanding of the parable or allegory?

6) Did the speaker give any explanation of any features of the parable or allegory?

7) What central truth or duty does the parable or allegory teach?

8) How did the teaching of the parable or allegory apply to the one(s) to whom it was given?

9) What application can we make of the parable or allegory to ourselves or to others to whom we minister?

10) In addition to what the parable or allegory teaches, does it illustrate any biblical truth other than what the speaker intended to convey?

11) If the parable or allegory was given by Jesus, what does it teach about Him?

(9) *Dispensational analysis* (Rule Nine)

1) To what dispensational section of the Scriptures does the passage to be interpreted belong?

2) To what dynamic age, if any, does the passage belong?

3) Does the passage address itself to some dispensational duty for the people to whom it belongs or to some event of the age to which it belongs?

4) While belonging to a section of Scripture that lies within the span of a certain dispensation or age, does the passage give duties or contain information about people or events relating to another dispensation or age?

5) If the passage does not lie within the scope of the Dispensation of Grace or the Church Age, does it give duty or illustrate some truth that can be applied to us today?

6) Is there any reference in the passage to one of the divine covenants? If so, what covenant is mentioned, what covenant promise is referred to, and to whom is it given?

(10) *Prophetic analysis* (Rule Ten)   Skip

1) Identify the prophetic portion, if any, in the passage to be interpreted.

2) Distinguish between the historical or contemporary events given in the passage and the future events that are predicted.

3) Recognize, identify, and interpret any figurative expression that may be found in the passage.

4) Study other biblical passages that refer to this prophecy; also, consider what the Bible as a whole teaches about this prophetic theme.

5) As objectively as possible, interpret the prophecy literally, in harmony with its context and the general teachings of Scripture.

6) When the prophecy allows more than one interpretation, choose the one that best fits the context and that presents the fewest interpretative problems.

7) Consider the possibility of multiple fulfillments of the prophecy. Identify these, if any, and determine what is the final fulfillment.

8) Seek to learn why the prophecy contributes to its context as well as to the biblical teaching of its theme.

9) Seek to learn by whom and to whom the prophecy was given.

10) Seek to learn what the prophecy contributes to its context as well as to the biblical teaching of its theme.

11) Determine if and how the prophecy relates to the Lord Jesus and to His first or second coming to earth or to His coming for the Church.

(11) *Doctrinal analysis* (Rule Eleven)

1) Recognize the doctrinal words that may be in the passage to be interpreted.

2) Look for any expressions of doctrinal concepts in the passage where their usual doctrinal words are missing or for which no special words occur in the Bible.

3) Identify the specific doctrines to which these words or concepts are related.

4) Observe how these words or concepts are related to these doctrines according to the general teachings of the Scriptures.

5) Consider how other passages in the Bible support or modify these doctrinal words or concepts.

6)   Observe what these words or concepts in the passage being interpreted say about these doctrines.

7)   Notice what these words or concepts contribute to the biblical teaching of these doctrines.

8)   Summarize the doctrinal teachings of the passage.

3. Interpretation and Organization of the Passage

(1) Enter the data you have gathered from your analyses into your verse charts (see Chapter 5, 1).

Do (2) Outline the organization of the passage (see Chapter 5, 2).

(3) Rewrite the passage, expressing your interpretation of it (see Chapter 5, 3).

(4) Consider how the passage, with your interpretation, contributes to the theme of the context and to the biblical teachings to which it refers.

4. Personal Application of the Passage

✓ (1)   Consider how the interpreted passage applies to your life and/or to that of others to whom you may minister (see Part Six).

✓ (2)   If one or more applications are present in the passage, choose an attainable spiritual goal for your life and set a time for your achieving it, with the Lord's help (Phil. 4:13).

(3)   Consider what new information the passage adds to your fund of Bible knowledge about God, the Lord Jesus Christ, or other biblical doctrines.

(4)   Consider what truth you may share with somebody today.

5. Prayer

Thank God for Himself, His Word, and what He has taught you. Ask Him for grace to translate the practical aspects of this truth into your life and through you unto others.

8

Additional Helps in Interpretation

In addition to the foregoing rules of interpretation, the following items may be helpful in interpreting the Bible.

1. An Understanding of Hebrew Parallelism

Biblical parallelism is a form of Hebrew poetry which reinforces a thought by repetition, contrast, or addition. This reinforcement often throws light on the meaning of the original thought. Consider the major kinds of parallelism.

(1) *Identical parallelism*

This reinforces the initial thought by repeating it, in part or in whole, with different words. The repetition of the initial thought often assists us in its interpretation by casting light on some aspect of it.

For example, Psalm 19:1 reads, "The heavens declare the glory of God; and the firmament shows His handiwork." Both statements speak of the celestial heavens. The second statement indicates that the glory of God is expressed by His handiwork— what He has made. The heavens express to us God's power, wisdom, and faithfulness. Thus the glory of God is some manifestation of the qualities of His divine nature.

In Psalm 22:16 we read: "For dogs have compassed me; the assembly of the wicked have inclosed me." This parallelism indicates that "dogs" refer to wicked people.

In Isaiah 55:6 we read, "Seek ye the LORD while He may be found; call ye upon Him while He is near." The second statement, "Call ye upon Him while He is near," shows what it means in this context to seek the LORD. It is to pray.

One must use caution in interpreting identical parallelism. There may be instances where the two statements do not refer to the same thing as in Luke 1:46-47. Mary said, "My soul does magnify the Lord, and my spirit has rejoiced in God my Savior." Since the Bible distinguishes between soul and spirit (Heb. 4:12), these may be separate components of our immaterial human nature. On the other hand, it is agreed that Mary extols God with her total being.

(2) *Antithetical parallelism*

This reinforces the initial thought by a contrasting statement. For example, Proverbs 15:1 says, "A soft answer turns away wrath; but grievous words stir up anger." This form of parallelism indicates that "a soft answer" not only turns away wrath but also does not provoke wrath.

We read in Psalm 1:6, "For the LORD knows the way of the righteous; but the way of the ungodly shall perish." The contrasting statement suggests that the LORD's knowing the way of the righteous not only refers to His awareness of their way but also to His prospering them in this way.

(3) *Climactic parallelism*

This form of parallelism adds to the initial thought. For example, Psalm 34:4 states, "I sought the LORD; and He heard me and delivered me from all my fears." These additional thoughts support the initial statement, "I sought the LORD," by describing the reward of seeking the LORD His hearing and delivering the speaker.

Hebrew parallelism is also found in the New Testament. For examples, see John 15:10; Romans 12:11; 13:14; 1 John 2:17.

2. Old Testament References in the New Testament

When comparing Old Testament references found in the New Testament with their original locations, one discovers that differences occur in their readings. How are these differences to be explained?[1]

(1) Since the New Testament writers were writing in Greek, they either translated the Old Testament references or used an existing Greek translation, such as the Septuagint (indicated by LXX). See Romans 10:11 where Paul quotes Isaiah 28:16 from the LXX.

(2) Sometimes the writers made a free translation of the Hebrew text. Compare Romans 9:27 with Isaiah 10:22.

(3) In certain cases, rather than referring to a single passage, the writer summarized the general teaching of the Old Testament Scriptures. See Matthew 2:23; John 1:45; Galatians 3:22.

(4) The writers often alluded to Old Testament passages without actually quoting them. See Acts 3:25 with Genesis 12:3; Acts 7:3 with Genesis 12:1; and 2 Corinthians 4:6 with Genesis 1:3.

(5) In giving the New Testament revelation, the Holy Spirit was free to make whatever changes in the Old Testament references that were needed to serve the divine purpose for the revelation of new truth. This does not mean that He changed the meaning of the Old Testament Scriptures. In their quotation in the New Testament, they were sometimes altered to support revelation of new truth. An author has the right to do this with his literary production.

When we read the Old Testament, we must avoid reading into these quoted Old Testament references the alterations that occur in their New Testament quotations. These Old Testament passages are to be interpreted in their original forms.

---

1. See Roger Nicole, "New Testament Use of the Old," in *Revelation and the Bible*, Carl F. H. Henry, ed. Grand Rapids: Baker Book House, ch. 9.

For a list of New Testament references to the Old Testament, see Manley, G. T. *The New Bible Handbook*. Downers Grove, IL: Inter-Varsity Press, 1951, pp. 442 ff.

3. The Golden Rule of Interpretation

"When the plain sense of Scripture makes common sense, seek no other sense; therefore, take every word at its primary, ordinary, usual, literal meaning unless the facts of the immediate context, studied in the light of related passages and axiomatic and fundamental truths, indicate clearly otherwise."[2]

4. Bible Chapter and Verse Divisions

The original writings did not have chapter and verse divisions as our Bibles do today. Thus, these divisions are not inspired. They were later added as an aid for turning to specific passages.

For purposes of interpretation, these divisions are sometimes mislocated when they interrupt the scriptural flow of a theme. Because of this, they should be ignored when one interprets the Scriptures. They serve only as reference indicators.

For example, the theme of Isaiah 53, "The Sufferings of the LORD's Servant," begins with 52:13. One should start here when interpreting this chapter.

5. The Dominant Theme of the Scriptures

When one interprets the Bible, he must keep in mind that the Lord Jesus Christ is its dominant theme (Luke 24:27, 44; John 1:45; 5:39). This was initiated by prophecy at the time of man's fall into sin (Gen. 3:15).

Christ's incarnation and atoning work are anticipated in the Old Testament by prophecy and types. They are accomplished in the Gospels. In the Acts the benefits of His sacrifice are applied to them who trusted Him and His atoning work. These truths are explained in the Epistles. And in the revelation they reach their highest point in the slain Lamb's standing before God's throne and in the visions of His judgments, second coming, millennial rule, and the establishment of the eternal state.

When we interpret the Bible, we should discover how the passage relates to the Lord Jesus. This relation may be expressed by prophecy, type, description, some activity, teaching, or exhortation. The Old Testament records His divine activities with the

---

2. David L. Cooper, *What Men Must Believe*, p. 63.

other members of the Trinity and looks forward to His incarnation. The New Testament largely deals with His incarnation and subsequent human activities, as the Servant of the Father. It also asserts His deity, as the Second Person of the Holy Trinity.

6. The Primary Names of God in the Scriptures

(1) In the Old Testament

In addition to the word "God," we find in the Old Testament two other primary designations for Deity which usually are represented by "LORD" and "Lord." For purposes of interpretation it is important to understand the meaning of these designations.

"God" is a generic name, representing kind of being. The Persons of the Trinity, the Father, Son, and Holy Spirit, have this designation and are God. In the Old Testament, "God" generally refers collectively to the Trinity (Gen. 1:1). This term is also used of false gods.

"LORD" (notice the capital letters) represents God's personal name. This, too, refers collectively to the Trinity, except in those passages where the context points to a specific Person of the Godhead (cp. Ps. 110:1, to God the Father). In the American Standard Version (1901), it is consistently translated "Jehovah." Many writers translate it "Yahweh." The Hebrew word consists of four consonants (YHWH), but how it is pronounced and what it means are not certain. This name does not mean Lord.

"Lord" is a title, representing the Hebrew word Adonai, meaning "My Master," or "My Ruler" (Isa. 6:1-12). Being a title, the word represents an office, or function. It means Lord.

In Psalm 110:1 we read, "The LORD said unto my Lord, Sit thou at my right hand until I make thine enemies thy footstool." With the above information in hand, the interpreter knows that "LORD" refers to God's personal name (in this case, God the Father); and "Lord" refers to God's title, "My Master" (in this case, the Lord Jesus). Under divine inspiration, David used "Lord" as a term of respect and of submission. See Matthew 22:41-46.

(2) In the New Testament

"Lord" (Greek: *Kurios*) in quotations from the Old Testament represents either Yahweh or Adonai, as determined by its original references and their contexts. When used in other passages, "Lord" seems to have a meaning similar to Adonai, for its Greek root suggests "One who has power (or authority)"; and the ancient translators of the Old Testament into Greek used *Kurios* for *Adonai.*

When used alone, "God" may refer collectively to the Trinity. However, it refers to God the Father in passages that also use designations for the Lord Jesus (1 Cor. 1:3-4). Exceptions to this rule occur in Ephesians 5:5; 2 Thessalonians 1:12; Titus 2:10, 13; and 2 Peter 1:1, where the Granville Sharp rule applies. In essence, this rule of Greek syntax states that when two nouns are joined by "and" and the first has the definite article but the second does not, then the latter always relates to the same person (or thing) as expressed by the first noun. In these occurrences Jesus is identified as being God. In each reference both proper nouns refer to Him.

Appendix A

The Parables and Allegories of Jesus

(in order of occurrence)

1. The Sign of the Temple (John 2:18-19)
2. The Physician (Luke 4:23) and the Prophet (v. 24)
3. The Bride and the Bridegroom (Matt. 9:14-15; Mark 2:19-20; Luke 5:34-35)
4. The New Cloth on an Old Garment (Matt. 9:16; Mark 2:21; Luke 5:36)
5. The New Wine in Old Wineskins (Matt. 9:17; Mark 2:22; Luke 5:37-39)
6. The Inward Light (Matt. 6:22-23; Luke 11:34-36)
7. The Wise and Foolish Builders (Matt. 7:24-27; Luke 6:46-49)
8. The Children of the Market Place (Matt. 11:16-19; Luke 7:29-35)
9. The Two Debtors (Luke 7:41-43)
10. Satan's Kingdom (Matt. 12:24-28; Mark 3:23-27)
11. The Return of the Unclean Spirit (Matt. 12:43-45)
12. The Sower and the Soils (Matt. 13:3-9, 18-23; Mark 4:1-9; Luke 8:4-8)
13. The Seed Growing of Itself (Luke 4:26-29)
14. The Wheat and the Weeds (Matt. 13:24-30, 36-43)

15. The Mustard Seed (Matt. 13:31-32; Mark 4:30-32; Luke
    13:18-19)
16. The Leaven (Matt. 13:33-35; Mark 4:33-34; Luke 13:21)
17. The Hidden Treasure (Matt. 13:44)
18. The Pearl of Great Price (Matt. 13:45-46)
19. The Fish Net (Matt. 13:47-50)
20. The Householder (Matt. 13:51-53)
21. The Unmerciful Servant (Matt. 18:21-35)
22. The Good Shepherd (John 10:1-6)
23. The Good Samaritan (Luke 10:30-37)
24. The Friend at Midnight (Luke 11:5-8)
25. The Rich Fool (Luke 12:13-21)
26. The Waiting and Watching Servants (Luke 12:35-38)
27. The Faithful and Wise Steward (Luke 12:41-48)
28. The Barren Fig Tree (Luke 13:6-9)
29. The Seating at the Marriage Feast (Luke 14:7-14)
30. The Great Supper (Luke 14:15-24)
31. The Unfinished Tower and the Unwaged War (Luke 14:25-34)
32. The Unsavory Salt (Luke 14:35)
33. The Lost Sheep (Luke 15:3-7)
34. The Lost Coin (Luke 15:810)
35. The Prodigal Son and the Elder Brother (Luke 15:11-32)
36. The Unrighteous Steward (Luke 16:1-13)
37. The Rich Man and Lazarus (Luke 16:19-31)
    While this passage is usually included with the parables,
    this actually is a historical event since a proper name is
    used.
38. The Unprofitable Servants (Luke 17:7-10)
39. The Unjust Judge and the Persistent Widow (Luke 18:1-8)
40. The Pharisee and the Publican (Luke 18:914)
41. The Laborers in the Vineyard (Matt. 20:1-16)
42. The Servants and the Pounds (Luke 19:11-27)
43. The Two Sons Called to Work (Matt. 21:28-32)
44. The Wicked Husbandmen (Matt. 21:33-41; Mark 12:1-9;
    Luke 2:9-16)
45. The Rejected Stone (Matt. 21:42-46; Mark 12:10-11; Luke
    20:17-19)
46. The Marriage Feast and the Wedding Garment (Matt. 22:1-
    14)

47. The Sprouting Fig Tree (Matt. 24:32-34; Mark 13:28-30; Luke 21:29-32)
48. The Householder and the Porter (Mark 13:34-37)
49. The Householder and the Thief (Matt. 24:43-44; Luke 12:39-40)
50. The Wise and Evil Servants (Matt. 24:45-51)
51. The Ten Virgins (Matt. 25:1-13)
52. The Servants and the Talents (Matt. 25:14-30)
53. The Sheep and the Goats (Matt. 25:31-46)
54. The Vine and the Branches (John 15:1-6)

Some brief parabolic illustrations

1. The Harvest Field (John 4:25-28)
2. Fishers of Men (Matt. 4:19; Mark 1:16-17; Luke 5:10)
3. The Salt of the Earth (Matt. 5:13)
4. The Light of the World (Matt. 5:14-16; Luke 11:34-36)
5. The Birds and the Flowers (Matt. 6:25-34; Luke 12:22-31)
6. Dogs and Swine (Matt. 7:6)
7. The Mote and the Beam (Matt. 7:1-5; Luke 6:41-42)
8. The Broad and the Narrow Ways (Matt. 7:13-14)
9. The Good and the Bad Fruit Trees (Matt. 7:16-20; Luke 6:43-45)
10. The Physician and the Sick (Matt. 9:12-13; Mark 2:17; Luke 5:31-32)
11. The Strong Man (Matt. 12:29-30; Mark 3:27; Luke 11:17-22)
12. The Good and Bad Treasures (Matt. 12:34-37)
13. The Unclean Spirit That Returned (Matt. 12:43-45; Luke 11:24-26)
14. Defilement (Matt. 15:10-11, 15-20; Mark 7:14-23)
15. Doomed Plants (Matt. 15:13)
16. The Blind Guiding the Blind (Matt. 15:14; Luke 6:39)
17. The Strait Gate and the Shut Door (Luke 13:23-30)
18. The Grain of Wheat (John 12:23-26)

Appendix B

Numbers, Colors, and Other Symbols

1. Numbers

Numbers in the Scriptures sometimes have symbolic meaning, especially when they are associated with other symbols, such as the tabernacle and its furnishings.

One—God (Deut. 6:4)
Two—divine witness, revelation (Deut. 17:6)
Three—the Trinity (Matt. 28:19; 1 John 5:7)
Four—the earth, the universe (Isa. 11:12; Matt. 24:31)
Five — divine grace (1 Sam. 17:40, 45-47)
Six—man, imperfection (Gen. 1:26-27, 31; Rev. 13:18)
Seven—spiritual perfection (Gen. 2:2-3; Rev. 5:6)
Eight — resurrection (Mark 16:2)
Nine—divine judgment (Mark 15:34)
Ten—completeness of order, legal perfection (Ex. 20:1-17)
Eleven — incompleteness (Acts 1:15-26)
Twelve — Israel, governmental perfection (Matt. 19:28)
Forty—divine testing, chastisement (Deut. 2:7; Heb. 3:9)

2. Colors

Black—sin (Job 24:13-16; 1 John 1:5-7)
Blue — Heaven, heavenly (an arbitrary meaning)
Green — grace (an arbitrary meaning)

Purple — royalty (Judg. 8:26; Mark 15:17-18)
Scarlet — blood, sacrifice (Lev. 17:11)
White — righteousness, righteous deeds (Rev. 19:8)

3. Metals

Brass (copper) — judgment (Rev. 1:15; 19:15; Ex. 27:1-2)
Gold—sovereignty (Dan. 2:37-38), Jesus' deity (an arbitrary
    meaning) (Ex. 26:29)
Iron — strength, conquest (Dan. 2:40)
Silver redemption (Lev. 27:1-25; Num. 18:15-16; Ex. 26:19)

4. Materials

Badger's skin—human nature, Jesus' humanity (an arbitrary
    meaning) (Ex. 26:14)
Goat's hair (black)—sin (Song 6:5; Lev. 16:21)
Linen — righteousness, righteous deeds (Rev. 19:8)
Olive oil—the Holy Spirit (1 Sam. 16:13)
Ram's skin dyed red — sacrifice, consecration (Lev. 8:18-30;
    Ex. 26:14)
Wood—human nature, Jesus' humanity (an arbitrary
    meaning) (Ex. 26:15)

Appendix C

Some Old Testament Types

1. Various Types of the Lord Jesus Christ

(1) Aaron: his priestly work (Heb. 7:11; 9:11-28).

(2) Abel: his sacrifice (Heb. 12:24; cp. Gen. 4:1-4).

(3) Adam: his being the head and pattern of the old human race; Christ, the head and pattern of the new humanity (1 Cor. 15:22, 45-49).

(4) Brazen Serpent: its being lifted up (Num. 21:9; John 3:14-15).

(5) Lamb: its being sacrificed (Ex. 29:38-42; John 1:29).

(6) Manna: its being eaten in the wilderness (Ex. 16:12-22; John 6: 30-56).

(7) Melchizedek: his person and his office as a priest-king (Gen. 14:18-20; Heb. 5:5-10).

(8) Moses: his being a prophet (Deut. 18:15, 18; Heb. 1:1-2) and his faithfulness (Heb. 3:1-6).

(9) Passover lamb: its being sacrificed and its blood applied (Ex. 12:1-28; 1 Cor. 5:7).

(10) Rock in the wilderness: its providing water (Ex. 17:6; 1 Cor. 10:4).

2. The Feasts of the LORD (Lev. 23)

(1) Feasts of Passover/Unleavened Bread (Lev. 23:4-8; 1 Cor. 5:7)

Passover was the first meal of this festive week, which

celebrated Israel's deliverance from the Death Angel and from Egyptian bondage. By His sacrifice the Lord Jesus, God's Lamb, delivers His people from bondage to sin and Satan as well as from divine judgment (Ex. ch. 12; Eph. 1:7; Cal. 1:13; 1 Thess. 1:10).

(2) Feast of Firstfruits (Lev. 23:9-14)

This anticipated the grain harvest by waving the first-fruits before the LORD. This was Israel's pledge to give God a tithe of the harvest and God's pledge to give the remaining harvest to Israel. Our Lord's resurrection was the firstfruits of all resurrections and the guarantee of all resurrections to follow (1 Cor. 15:20-23).

(3) Feast of Weeks (Pentecost) (Lev. 23:15-22)

This celebrated the barley harvest. It typically portrays the coming of the Holy Spirit on the Day of Pentecost and Christ's special harvest of Gentiles during the present age in His build-ing the Church (Acts 15:13-17).

(4) Feast of Trumpets (Lev. 23:23-25)

Trumpets were used to convey signals to the people of Israel (Num. 10:1-10). Among these signals were those which notified the people when they were to gather and to worship (vv. 7-8, 10). This feast typically anticipates the time when the Lord Jesus will return and will gather the elect of Israel to their promised land (Deut. 30:1-5; Matt. 24:31).

(5) Feast of Tabernacles (Lev. 23:33-43)

This celebrated God's care of Israel during their wilder-ness journey and His giving them crops during the previous agricultural season. Typically, it anticipates the blessings of Christ's earthly, millennial reign as well as His care for His peo-ple during their pilgrimage through this world (Isa. 11:1-10; 1 Peter 2:11; 4:19).

3. The Day of Atonement (Lev. 23:26-32; 16:1-34)

This was the day when the high priest offered sacrifice for the sins of Israel and himself. The Lord Jesus gave Himself once-for-all in atonement for the sins of His people (Heb. 9:11-15).

4. The Tabernacle in the Wilderness

  (1) Its fence and gate (Ex. 27:9-19)
Jesus alone is the way to God (John 14:6).

  (2) Its framework (Ex. 26:15-30)
Wood covered with gold portrays Jesus' human and divine natures (John 1:1, 14).

  (3) Its coverings (Ex. 26:1-14)
These depict our Lord's character and atoning work (see Appendix B).

  (4) Its brazen altar (Ex. 27:1-8)
This is typical of the cross and of our Lord's sacrifice upon it (1 Cor. 1:18).

  (5) Its laver (Ex. 30:17-21)
This speaks of divine cleansing from sin (Acts 10:43; 1 John 1:7, 9).

  (6) Its outer veil (Ex. 26:36-37)
The only approach to God is through the Lord Jesus (John 14:6; Eph. 2:18).

  (7) Its lampstand (Ex. 25:31-40)
The Lord Jesus is the light of the world (John 8:12). His people are light in Him (Eph. 5:8), reflecting His light to the world.

  (8) Its table of showbread (Ex. 25:23-30; Lev. 24:5-9)
The Lord Jesus is the bread of life (John 6:35).

  (9) Its altar of incense (Ex. 30:1-10)
The Lord Jesus is our intecessor (Heb. 7:25).

  (10) Its inner veil (Ex. 26:31-35)
With Jesus' sacrifice the inner veil that separated the worshiper from God was rent (Matt. 27:51). We now have free access to God through Him (Heb. 10:19-22).

  (11) Its ark of the covenant (Ex. 25:10-16)
This contained Israel's holy relics (Heb. 9:4). The Lord Jesus is the repository of the fullness of God and of our spiritual blessings (Col. 1:19; Eph. 1:3).

(12) Its mercy seat (Ex. 25:17-22)

The lid of the ark, called "the mercy seat," was the place where the atoning blood was sprinkled annually (Lev. 16:14). It also was the place where God met with the high priest, the representative of the people (Ex. 25:22).

The cross was the place where the divine atonement was made in the person of the Lord Jesus for our sins (1 Peter 2:24; 3:18). He also was our propitiation (1 John 2:2), the divine sacrifice that placated God's wrath against us. He now continually represents us before God (v. 1).

5. The Levitical Offerings

(1) The burnt offering (Lev. 1; 6:8-13)

A sweet savor offering, the blood was caught and sprinkled upon the altar. The skinned carcass was divided and wholly consumed by fire. This typically portrays our Lord's complete dedication to the Father's will, even unto death (John 6:38; Phil. 2:8).

(2) The meal offering (Lev. 2; 6:14-18)

A sweet savor offering, this consisted of fine flour, olive oil, frankincense, and salt. These ingredients portray various aspects of our Lord's human character: the flour, His perfections (John 1:14); the olive oil, His power in the Holy Spirit (Acts 10:38); the frankincense, His delight to the Father (Matt. 3:17); and the salt, His sinlessness (1 Peter 2:22; 1 John 3:5).

(3) The peace offering (Lev. 3; 7:11-18)

A sweet savor offering, this consisted of the animal's blood being sprinkled upon the altar and its fat being consumed by fire. The rest of the flesh was eaten by the offerer and his friends.

The blood portrays our Lord's life given in death (Col. 1:20-22); and the burned fat, His satisfying God's demands against us (Eph. 5:2). The eating of the flesh represents our receiving Him for reconciliation with God (Rom. 5:1, 10-11), our access to God through Him, and our union with others in Him (Eph. 2:13-18).

(4) The sin offering (Lev. 4; 6:24-30)

This consisted of a ritual with the animal's blood, the burning of its fat on the altar, and the burning of the carcass outside the camp. This dealt more with sins against God, such as those of ignorance and ceremonial infractions. This portrays Christ as our sin-bearer, dying in our place to pay the awful debt of our sins (1 Peter 2:24; Heb. 13:12).

(5) The trespass offering (Lev. 5:1—6:7; 7:1-10; 19:20-22)

This consisted of the sprinkling of the animal's blood upon the altar and the consumption of its fat by fire. This dealt more with sins against man, such as those of deception, misappropriation, and passion. Again, the Lord Jesus was our substitute, paying by His death the debt of our sins (1 Cor. 15:3; Rom. 5:8).

Appendix D
Some Useful Books for Interpreting the Bible

ATLAS AND GEOGRAPHY

Aharoni, Yohann, and Aini-Yonah, Michael. *The Macmillan Bible Atlas*. New York: Macmillan, 1977.

Bay, Denis. *The Geography of the Bible*. New York: Harper and Row, revised, 1974.

Pfeiffer, Charles Franklin, ed. *Baker's Bible Atlas*. Grand Rapids: Baker Book House, revised edition, 1973.

CONCORDANCE

The New American Standard Exhaustive Concordance. Nashville: Holman Bible Publishers.

The New International Version Complete Concordance. Grand Rapids: Zondervan Publishing House.

The New King James Version Complete Concordance. Nashville: Thomas Nelson.

Strong, James. *Exhaustive Concordance of the Bible*. (KJV) Nashville: Abingdon, revised edition, 1980.

Young, Robert. *Analytical Concordance to the Bible*. (KJV) Grand Rapids: Wm. B. Eerdmans Publishing Co., 1955.

Walker, J.B.R. *Walker's Comprehensive Bible Concordance*. Grand Rapids, Kregel Publications, 1976.

Wigram, George V. *The Englishman's Greek Concordance of the New Testament.* Grand Rapids: Wm. B. Eerdmans Publishing Co.

――――――. *The Englishman's Hebrew and Chaldee Concordance of the Old Testament.* Grand Rapids: Wm. B. Eerdmans Publishing Co.

CROSS-REFERENCE

The Treasury of Scripture Knowledge. Old Tappan, NJ: Fleming H. Revell.

CUSTOMS

Thompson, J. A. *Handbook of Life in Bible Times.* Downers Grove, IL.: InterVarsity Press.

Wight, Fred H. *Manners and Customs of Bible Lands.* Chicago: Moody Press, 1953.

Wight, Fred H. & Gower, Ralph. *The New Manners and Customs of Bible Times.* Chicago: Moody Press.

DICTIONARY, ENCYCLOPEDIA, HANDBOOK

Alexander, David and Pat, eds. *Eerdman's Handbook to the Bible.* Grand Rapids: Wm. B. Eerdmans Publishing Co., 1973.

Halley, Henry H. *Halley's Bible Handbook.* Grand Rapids: Zondervan Publishing House.

Lockyer, Herbert, Sr. *Nelson's Illustrated Bible Dictionary.* Nashville: Thomas Nelson, 1986.

Packer, James I., ed. *The Bible Almanac.* Nashville: Thomas Nelson.

Tenney, Merrill C., ed. *Zondervan Pictorial Encyclopedia of the Bible.* Grand Rapids: Zondervan Publishing House.

Unger, Merrill F. *Unger's Bible Handbook.* Chicago: Moody Press, 1966.

DISPENSATIONALISM

Ryrie, Charles C. *Dispensationalism Today.* Chicago: Moody Press.

FIGURES OF SPEECH

Bullinger, E. W. *Figures of Speech Used in the Bible.* Grand Rapids: Baker Book House.

Bullinger, E. W. *Number in Scripture.* Grand Rapids: Kregel Publications, 1967.

HISTORY

Bruce, F. F. *New Testament History*. Garden City: Doubleday, 1972.

Edersheim, Alfred. *The Life and Times of Jesus the Messiah*. Grand Rapids: Wm. B. Eerdmans Publishing Co.

Harrison, Roland Kenneth. *Old Testament Times*. Grand Rapids: Wm. B. Eerdmans Publishing Co.

Pfieffer, Charles. *Old Testament History*. Grand Rapids: Baker Book House.

INTRODUCTION

Archer, Gleason. *A Survey of Old Testament Introduction*. Chicago: Moody Press, 1974.

Geisler, Norman L., and Nix, William E. *A General Introduction to the Bible*. Chicago: Moody Press, 1968.

Guthrie, Donald. *Introduction to the New Testament*. Downers Grove, Ill.: Inter-Varsity Press, 1970.

Harrison, Roland Kenneth. *Introduction to the Old Testament*. Grand Rapids: Wm. B. Eerdmans Publishing Co., 1969.

Scroggie, W. Graham. *The Unfolding Drama of Redemption*. Grand Rapids: Zondervan, 1972.

Tenney, Merrill C. *New Testament Survey*. Grand Rapids: Wm. B. Eerdmans Publishing Co., revised edition, 1961.

Thiessen, Henry C. *Introduction to the New Testament*. Grand Rapids: Wm. B. Eerdmans Publishing Co., 1943.

Unger, Merill F. *Introductory Guide to the Old Testament*. Grand Rapids: Zondervan, revised edition.

Young, Edward J. *An Introduction to the Old Testament*. Grand Rapids: Wm. B. Eerdmans Publishing Co., 1949.

PROPHECY

Girdlestone, R. B. *The Grammar of Prophecy*. Grand Rapids: Kregel Publications, 1955.

Pentecost, J. Dwight. *Things to Come*. Grand Rapids: Zondervan Publishing House.

Tan, Paul. *The Interpretation of Prophecy*. Winona Lake, IN: BMH, 1974.

Walvoord, John. Various writings. Grand Rapids: Zondervan Publishing House.

TOPICS

Inglis, James. *Compact Topical Bible*. Grand Rapids: Kregel Publications, 1990.

Nave's Topical Bible. Various publishers.

TYPOLOGY

Soltau, Henry W. *The Holy Vessels and the Furniture of the Tabernacle*. Grand Rapids: Kregel Publications, 1971.

—————. *The Tabernacle; the Priesthood and the Offerings*. Grand Rapids: Kregel Publications, 1972.

WORD STUDY

Detzler, Wayne A.: *New Testament Words in Today's Language*. Wheaton: Victor Books, 1986.

Richards, Lawrence O. *Expository Dictionary of Bible Words*. Grand Rapids: Zondervan Publishing House.

Unger, Merrill F. and White, William, Jr. *Nelson's Expository Dictionary of the Old Testament*. Nashville: Thomas Nelson, 1980.

Vine, W. E. *Expository Dictionary of Old Testament and New Testament Words*. Old Tappan, N. J.: Fleming H. Revell, 1981.

Wuest, Kenneth S. *New Testament Word Studies*. Grand Rapids: Wm. B. Eerdmans Publishing Co.

Appendix E
The Vocabulary of Prophecy

In the prophetic passages of the Bible certain words and phrases have special meanings. Some of these follow:

Betrothal, marriage

A covenant alliance between Israel and God (Jer. 31:32; Hos. 2).

Day of Christ

This refers to the time when the Lord Jesus will come and remove the Church from the earth (1 Cor. 1:8; 5:5; Phil. 1:6, 10; 2:16; 2 Thess. 2:2). This will occur at the close of the present Church Age.

Day of the Lord

This is a period of time that extends from the rapture of the Church (2 Thess. 2:2) until the dissolution of the universe (2 Peter 3:10) at the time of the Great White Throne Judgment (Rev. 20:11). In the Scriptures the Day of the Lord refers to events that take place during this span of time rather than to the entire period itself. (See 1 Thess. 5:1-9; 2 Thess. 2:1-3 *Grk.*; Joel 1:15; 2:1-11, 28-32; 3:14; Amos 5:18, 26; Zeph. 1:7—2:3; Isa. 13:6-16; 2 Peter 3:10).

Fire, burning

This can represent divine judgment (Jer. 4:4; Mal. 4:1).

119

Harlotry, divorce
This represents the breaking of the covenant alliance by God's people committing idolatry (Hos. 1:2; 4:17-18; Jer. 3:8).

In the last days, the latter days, time of the end
This seems to refer to the last days of the Jewish Age (the 70 weeks of Daniel 9) when God will deal with the elect of Israel and they will be saved and be restored to their land (Isa. 2:2; Mic. 4:1; Hos. 3:5; Dan. 11:40; 12:4).

Kingdom of God
Prophetically, this refers to our Lord's millennial earthly reign (Dan. 2:44; Ps. 2:6-9; Rev. 11:15). In 1 Corinthians 15:24-28, it refers to God's future universal kingdom which will continue forever.

North
This direction can represent any country that is approximately north of Palestine, such as Assyria (Zech. 2:13), Babylon (Jer. 46:10), Media-Persia (Jer. 50:9), Syria, the area out of which the Beast out of the Sea (Rev. 13:1-3) will rise (Dan. 8:9; 11:21-45).

Return
This signifies repentance, a change of mind, leading to a change of moral, or spiritual, direction (Deut. 30:2; Hos. 3:5).

River
This can represent a lot of people (Isa. 8:7).

Sea
This can represent a multitude of people (Jer. 51:42).

South
This direction can represent Egypt, which is south of Palestine (Dan. 11:5, 9, 11, 14, 25, 40).

Turning of captivity
The deliverance of Israel from her enemies and her restoration to her land (Deut. 30:3; Jer. 30:3; 31:23; 33:7, 26).

Appendix F

The Meaning of Biblical Hermeneutics

According to Greek Mythology, the god Hermes (the Roman Mercury, Acts 14:12) was the messenger of the gods. He was sent to make plain the will of the gods to men. He brought the divine messages and explained them to men.

Essentially, hermeneutics is the science of the laws and principles of literary interpretation and explanation. The word comes from the Greek verb *hermeneuo*, meaning: (1) to explain something to someone (LXX, Esther 10:3) and (2) to translate something, that is, to put a text into another language (John 1:42; 9:7; Heb. 7:2). Other related verbs are *diermeneuo*, an intensified form of *hermeneuo*, meaning: (1) to explain something (Luke 24:27; 1 Cor. 12:30; 14:5, 13, 27) and (2) to translate something (Acts 9:36); and *methermeneuo*, which always means to translate from one language to another (Matt. 1:23; Mark 5:41; 15:22, 34; John 1:41; Acts 4:36; 13:8).

While biblical hermeneutics is the art of interpreting the Scriptures, biblical exegesis is the practical exposition of the meaning of the Scriptures. Exegesis comes from the Greek verb *exegeomai*, meaning to lead (cp. Luke 24:35; Acts 10:8; 15:14; 21:19). Thus we use the rules of hermeneutics to arrive at an understanding of a Bible passage; and we pass on this understanding to others by biblical exegesis, or exposition.

Usually, a distinction is made between general hermeneutics and special hermeneutics. General hermeneutics applies to all kinds of literary works. It consists of those rules that relate to context, the meaning of words, grammar, background, and figurative expressions. Special hermeneutics has rules that apply to special kinds of literary works such as biblical types, parables, allegories, Hebrew poetry, and prophecy.

Appendix G
Kinds of Bibles

1. According to Their English Translations

(1) Literal Translations

These are largely word-for-word translations of the Bible from the original languages into English. These are most desirable for serious Bible study.

Examples are *The King James Version, The New King James Version, The American Standard Version* (1901), and *The New American Standard Version.*

(2) Idiomatic Translations

These are clause-for-clause translations, made with an effort to give the ideas expressed by the original language in modern, informal English.

An example is *The New Testament in Modern English* by J. B. Phillips.

(3) Combined Translations

These are translations that are partly literal and partly idiomatic.

Examples are the New English Bible and the New International Version.

(4) Expanded Translations

Since single biblical Hebrew and Greek words cannot always be fully expressed by single English words, an effort is made in these expanded translations to express more completely the meaning or force of the words in the original languages.

Examples are *An Expanded Translation of the New Testament* by Kenneth Wuest and *The Amplified Bible*.

(5) Simplified Translations

The purpose of these is to reach a wider readership by providing a Bible with the simplest vocabulary of spoken, informal English.

An example of this is *Today's English Version* by Robert Bratcher.

(6) Paraphrased Translations

To paraphrase is to say the same thing in other words. While any translation requires some paraphrasing, this kind of translation is almost wholly paraphrased. Since a paraphrase is essentially an interpretation of the Scriptures, the value of this kind of translation rests upon the accuracy of the author's interpretation. This kind of translation is not desirable for one who seeks his own interpretation of the Scriptures.

An example is *The Living Bible* by Kenneth N. Taylor.

(7) Biased Translations

These are translations, often produced by the cults, which strongly incorporate and reflect the translator's theological bias.

Examples are *The Revised Standard Version*, which sometimes reflects the religious liberalism of its translators; *The New World Bible*, which reflects the doctrines of the Jehovah's Witnesses; and *The Revised King James Version*, which reflects the doctrines of Mormonism.

2. According to Their Content

(1) The Text Bible

This kind of Bible has only the text of Scripture.

(2) The Reference Bible

This kind of Bible has center-column and/or marginal references to other passages, translations of original words, and the like.

(3) The Teacher's Bible

This is a reference Bible which has a supplement that contains helps for teachers such as maps, an outline of the life of Jesus, a list of His parables, biblical weights and measures, a brief concordance, and other useful material.

(4) The Annotated Bible

This is a reference Bible that has an introduction and outline of each biblical book as well as editorial comments on and explanations of biblical passages, words, and doctrines.

Among the many that exist today are the *Scofield Reference Bible* and the *Ryrie Study Bible*.

Condensed Translation
    Author deletes parts

Other Books for Profitable Bible Study

THE COMPANION BIBLE

Notes and appendices by E. W. Bullinger. The Most Complete One-volume Study Bible Available in the King James Version! Notes within the text give valuable insight into the original Greek and Hebrew languages. Alternate translations, explanations of figures of speech, cross-references and an introductory detailed outline of each book and chapter are among the many features which pastors, preachers, seminarians and Bible students will find helpful.

Additional helps include:

- 198 appendices including explanations of Hebrew words and their use, charts, parallel passages, maps, lists of proper names, calendars, timelines, etc. Notes are keyed to these indexes.
- Distinguishing type used for divine names and titles.
- Archaeological findings and historical genealogies.
- Factual marginal notes.

ISBN 0-8254-2203-5	2,160 pp.	deluxe hardcover
ISBN 0-8254-2288-4	2,160 pp.	bonded leather

HOW TO ENJOY THE BIBLE   E. W. Bullinger

A unique introduction to your study of God's Word. E. W. Bullinger guides you in the adventure of open and honest study of the Scripture from within—allowing it to speak for itself. Twelve practical principles of interpretation make inductive Bible study come alive! *How to Enjoy the Bible* establishes the integrity and trustworthiness of the Scripture based on its own internal evidence. All believers will be encouraged in their discovery of how to read, study, and enjoy the sacred contents of the Bible.

ISBN 0-8254-2213-2	466 pp.	paperback
ISBN 0-8254-2287-6	466 pp.	deluxe hardcover

NUMBER IN SCRIPTURE   E. W. BULLINGER

An invaluable guide to the study of biblical Numerology, or Numerics. The first section reveals the amazing designs of the numbers and numerical features of the Word of God which give evidence to their Designer. The second section highlights the spiritual significance and symbolical connotations of numbers which are repeated in different contexts throughout the Bible.

This thrilling and provocative study will provide a storehouse of knowledge and ideas for ministers, teachers and Bible students.

ISBN 0-8254-2238-8   212 pp.   paperback

THE NEW COMPACT TOPICAL BIBLE   James Inglis

The perfect Bible companion for beginning Bible students and a handy reference for pastors and teachers, *The Compact Topical Bible* is an easy-to-use treasure house of Scripture information.

Inglis provides a complete collection of Scripture verses arranged under a comprehensive, alphabetical list of Bible subjects. All subjects found in the Bible, whether doctrinal, devotional, practical, ecclesiastical, biographical, or secular, are included.

The result is a master reference for quick and accurate Bible study, allowing the Scriptures to speak for themselves on topics from A to Z. All Bible students will find *The Compact Topical Bible* a trustworthy, "user-friendly" tool for discovering the wonderful truths of God's Word.

ISBN 0-8254-2900-5   528 pp.   paperback

JONES' DICTIONARY OF OLD
TESTAMENT PROPER NAMES   Alfred Jones

A complete dictionary of the names occurring in the Old Testament arranged in English alphabetical order. Jones provides the Hebrew or Aramaic equivilents and explains their meanings according to the original languages. This thorough reference on Old Testament names is now keyed to *Strong's Exhaustive Concordance.*

Jones describes 3,600 names representing 16,500 individuals or places with archaeological and etymological information, making this the standard reference for every Bible student's library.

ISBN 0-8254-2961-7   382 pp.   paperback
ISBN 0-8254-2962-5   382 pp.   deluxe hardcover

NUMBERS IN THE BIBLE   Robert D. Johnston

Numbers in the Bible offers a fascinating investigation of biblical numerology. Johnston includes an insightful presentation of the accuracy of scriptural numerics, the perfection of the Son of God in numerical ways, and a chapter on deepening your own private study of this subject. The reader will find both profit and inspiration from this intriguing study.

ISBN 0-8254-3628-1   112 pp.   paperback

I Love my wife Robin.   *I Love my fiancée M*